For Sue.

Fondly, Abm

# Poverty, work, and freedom

The poor seem easy to identify: those who do not have enough money or enough of the things money can buy. This book explores a different approach to poverty, one suggested by the notion of capabilities that is emphasized by Amartya Sen and Martha Nussbaum. In the spirit of the capabilities approach, the book argues that poverty refers not to a lack of things but to the lack of the ability to live life in a particular way. However, rather than seeking to identify a prescribed set of activities and ways of being that are necessary for a fully human life, the book focuses attention on a particular capability, the capability for creative living, and explores the idea that we might consider poverty to be the inability to live creatively. The authors argue that the poor are those who cannot live a life that is discovered and created rather than already known. Avoiding poverty means having the capacity and opportunity to achieve this type of living. The authors argue that the capacity to do skilled work plays a particularly important role in creative living, and suggest that the development of the ability to do skilled work is a vital part of solving the problem of poverty.

DAVID P. LEVINE is Professor of Economics at the Graduate School of International Studies, University of Denver. He has published numerous articles and nine books in economics and political economy, most recently *Normative Political Economy: Subjective Freedom, the Market and the State* (2001). He has also published in the field of applied psychoanalysis.

S. ABU TURAB RIZVI is Associate Professor at the Department of Economics, University of Vermont. His research, concerning microeconomics and its history, has been published in the *Cambridge Journal of Economics*, *History of Political Economy*, and the *Review of Political Economy*.

# Poverty, work, and freedom

*Political economy and the moral order*

David P. Levine
*University of Denver*

S. Abu Turab Rizvi
*University of Vermont*

CAMBRIDGE
UNIVERSITY PRESS

CAMBRIDGE UNIVERSITY PRESS
Cambridge, New York, Melbourne, Madrid, Cape Town, Singapore, São Paulo

Cambridge University Press
The Edinburgh Building, Cambridge, CB2 2RU, UK

Published in the United States of America by Cambridge University Press,
New York

www.cambridge.org
Information on this title: www.cambridge.org/9780521848268

First published 2005

Printed in the United Kingdom at the University Press, Cambridge

*A catalogue record for this book is available from the British Library*

*Library of Congress cataloguing in publication data*

ISBN-13 978-0-521-84826-8 hardback
ISBN-10 0-521-84826-1 hardback

Cambridge University Press has no responsibility for the persistence or
accuracy of URLs for external or third-party internet websites referred to in
this book, and does not guarantee that any content on such websites is, or will
remain, accurate or appropriate.

# Contents

# Preface

We speak about the poor as if we know who they are. We speak, for example, as if the arbitrary definitions used by government agencies to determine eligibility for their programs tell us who is poor and who is not. If we know who are the poor, the problem is what, if anything, to do about them. For some, knowing what to do about poverty means becoming an advocate for the poor, or for what their interests are imagined to be. Then, the problem becomes one of representation of interests, and possibly of the struggle on behalf of those interests against the interests of those who are not poor and whose interests might be opposed to the interests of the poor.

Sometimes we speak about poverty as if it were defined by wealth. The poor are those who do not have enough wealth. This is the approach taken by Adam Smith in the first paragraphs of *The Wealth of Nations*, where he defines the problem of political economy as the problem of wealth and poverty. When we speak this way, poverty often becomes a relative matter; the more wealth on average in our society, the more wealth we need to avoid being poor. This way of thinking about poverty makes it an implication of inequality, which, for some, makes poverty a problem of injustice. This follows if we convince ourselves that those who have less (and therefore are poor) do so because others have more. If the rich become rich by exploiting the poor, then what makes some wealthy makes others poor.

Yet, we will not get very far in understanding poverty by starting with the poor and seeking to identify their shared interests and characteristics. This is because attempting to do so assumes that we already know what an inquiry into poverty is meant to find out: what it is we lack that makes us poor, and therefore who is poor and who is not. Our purpose in writing this book is to explore the idea of poverty so that we can come to know better what it means to be poor, and therefore who is and who is not poor.

Our concern, then, is not with the empirical description of poverty, but with the idea of poverty. The idea of poverty is the idea of something that is missing. To be poor is to lack this something. But everyone lacks something; so an idea of poverty depends on a judgment about the things we might lack. This judgment tells us when not having something leaves us poor. The judgment involved here cannot be made empirically since it is meant to guide us in our effort to understand experience. It can only be made on the basis of an idea about living that tells us what we need to lead a life of a particular kind. This makes any effort to define poverty a matter of norms or ideals.

Appeal to ideals of living might seem to take us onto terrain just as arbitrary as the terrain on which we began: the arbitrary definition of poverty as a level of income designated by a government agency. Reference to norms can be arbitrary, especially if those making the reference do little more than project their own personal values onto others, or, in a more collective spirit, seek to compile a list of valued and necessary life activities based on what is valued by the community.

Our approach is meant to avoid the arbitrary specification of a level of income, a living standard, or a set of life activities. In place of these ideas, we offer the simple premise that, so far as we respect individual freedom, we cannot know in advance what makes any particular individual's life worthwhile, because what makes a life worthwhile in a society of individuals remains to be determined by those individuals themselves. Our problem is how to conceive poverty in a way consistent with this premise. This is the central problem we need to solve if we are to have an idea of poverty applicable to a modern society. Our task, then, is to answer questions such as these: Can we have a meaningful notion of poverty that respects self-determination? Can we conceive poverty in a way that incorporates into our ideal of living the condition that we do not know what others need to have and to do to make their lives meaningful? We can only respect freedom if we drop the assumption that answers to questions about living can be provided for rather than by the individual. We must, in other words, start from not knowing and the unknown rather than from what is already known.

We attempt to develop a notion of poverty consistent with the ideal of freedom by considering what demands are placed on the individual by the absence of predetermination of ends. We speak of the ideal of freedom in the language of creativity and creative living, of a life devoted to exploring, in the words of Erik Erikson, opportunities yet to be determined. We argue that what people need to live a life that is not predetermined is not particular goods, a specific standard of living, or the capability to engage in a predetermined set of activities, but instead the capacity and opportunity to discover and to create. We try to indicate as concretely as we can what it means to have the capacity to discover and to create. We consider someone poor in a society committed to the ideal of freedom when he or she lacks this capacity or the opportunity to exercise it.

We do not argue that the ideal of freedom as the capacity to discover and create is the only reasonable ideal that could be applied to the problem of conceiving poverty; nor do we insist that this ideal is inherently the best among a set of competing options. We do, however, suggest that this ideal is uniquely relevant to the world in which we find ourselves, and, more importantly, has a special power in that world to make alternatives unconvincing and inapplicable.

This special power is the power of individual difference. Older ideals derive their power from that of the group and the norms embedded in the group's cultural reality. This group-based cultural reality is also a moral reality or moral order. Freedom and individual self-determination rest uneasily in a moral order, since a moral order consists of already known and predetermined ways of life. The moral order is not open to opportunities yet to be determined; it subsumes the individual self into the group self rather than offering the individual a facilitating environment for self-development.

The power of the norms that constitute a moral order derives from the group's ability to require compliance as a condition of membership and from its ability to make membership the only path to moral standing. But, in a world where many groups must coexist, and where the individual can exist outside the group, the power of the group to control access to moral standing weakens. After all, there are other groups with different notions of the good life, and there are individuals who define the good life outside the group. Thus, the power of the ideal of creative living derives from the power of the ideal of individual freedom to undermine the hold the group has over its members.

The role of groups bears on whether we consider poverty a matter of injustice. If some are denied access to the opportunity to develop and exercise the capacity for creative living because they are ascribed membership in groups independently of their will (groups based, for example, on such characteristics as race, ethnicity, and gender), then we can consider injustice a primary cause of their poverty. This is in part the injustice that inevitably follows when individual self-determination is sacrificed to group identification. Denial of individual self-determination is, of course, only an injustice when the idea of justice is grounded in individual self-determination.

The issue, then, has to do primarily with the norm that governs the relationship between the individual and the group. In a modern society, which is to say a society organized around the ideal of freedom, we cannot escape from poverty unless we can escape from ascribed group identification, although our ability to do so does not in itself guarantee we will not be poor. Still, the struggle over poverty is a struggle for individual identity.

The problem of poverty in a modern setting not only concerns what it means to be poor when needs and activities are no longer predetermined, it is also the problem of how regard for others can be consistent with the breakdown of the moral order and its replacement by a society of individuals. This latter has a bearing on the question alluded to above: Assuming we can determine what it means to be poor, what, if anything, needs to be done about the condition of those who are poor? Is a society of individuals in any way compelled to be concerned about those who fail to realize the ideal on which it is founded? At the end of our study of poverty, we consider how we might answer this question in the affirmative, and how regard for others might develop outside the moral order.

Though we may still apply a notion of justice as freedom to the problem of poverty, thinking about poverty in the way we suggest tends to remove it from the terrain of inequality and justice, placing it instead on the terrain of capability and opportunity. These are no doubt overlapping regions, but they are not the same space. We wrote this book in part out of a conviction that poverty is a much more important question than inequality and therefore a more important question than justice defined on the basis of equality. Put another way, we seek to focus attention on poverty and the poor rather than on the relationship between those who are poor and those who are not. We do so on the grounds that if you are poor your problem is that you lack something vital for living. This does not become a problem because others have what you do not; it is a problem regardless of the circumstances in which others find themselves.

# Acknowledgments

Some material included here was originally published in the *American Behavioral Scientist,* vol. 43, no. 2 (October 1999), the *Review of Political Economy* vol. 16, no. 1 (January 2004), and by the University of Denver as The University Lecture (Denver 2004). Preliminary versions of ideas developed in the book were presented at the University of Vermont, the University of New South Wales, and St. Michael's College (Vermont).

Abu Rizvi would like to thank Elaine McCrate, Stephanie Seguino, Ross Thomson, and Jaafar Rizvi for helpful discussions. He would like to dedicate his contribution to this volume to his father and to the memory of his mother.

# 1    Introduction

What is the essential thing that we lack when we are poor? Answers to this question often refer to a set of goods, basic needs, or a minimum level of income. Despite their differences, these concepts all connect to a long-standing tradition of thinking in political economy that emphasizes the idea of subsistence. The idea of poverty as the lack of subsistence has played a central role in political economy since the first pages of the *Wealth of Nations*, where Adam Smith distinguishes between what he calls the civilized and savage states of man on the basis of the "abundance or scantiness" of the supply of the "necessities and conveniences of life" annually consumed.

However straightforward we might imagine this idea to be, even for the classical economists it turned out to involve complexities. Thus, we find the classical theorists using the term subsistence in two significantly different senses (see Levine 1998: ch. 1). According to the first, subsistence refers to needs associated with maintaining the physical integrity of the human organism, natural needs of human beings considered part of a natural order. According to the second, subsistence refers to needs associated with a culturally and historically determined way of life. The first account makes poverty a threat to the organism's physical survival; the second makes it a threat to its cultural survival. The two threats need not, of course, be entirely separate matters. Yet, neither are they the same, and defining poverty as a threat to physical survival has importantly different implications from those that follow when we define poverty as cultural deprivation.

While this distinction is important, so also is the feature shared by the two notions of subsistence. Both encourage us to think about poverty as failure to satisfy a set of well-defined and predetermined needs. Because of this, we can say that the notion of subsistence, whether physical or cultural, leads us in the direction of what we might refer to as a prescriptive theory of poverty. By a prescriptive theory, we have in mind a theory that requires a prior specification of a set of needs. Poverty then means failure to satisfy the prescribed set of needs.[1]

It would seem that the simplest way to prescribe needs would be to begin with physical subsistence, consisting of the organism's elemental or basic physiological needs for food, water, shelter, and so on. Yet, even were we able to identify such a set of basic needs, and doing so is no simple matter, serious obstacles stand in the way of our attempt to apply this idea to the problem of defining poverty. Specification of basic needs does not tell us how they are to be satisfied. It matters how the nutrients are delivered, what sort of shelter is provided, how broadly or narrowly the organism is conceived and therefore how broadly or narrowly the physical subsistence must also be conceived. All of these considerations give us reason for skepticism about the usefulness of taking physical need as our starting point, a matter discussed further in Chapter 4.

The difficulties involved in defining basic needs may, indeed, be intractable, but the more fundamental failing of this approach to defining poverty is that it does not allow us to consider poor anyone whose basic needs are satisfied no matter how that satisfaction is provided. Yet, surely anyone who has only his or her basic needs satisfied is by that very fact poor, which tells us that an adequate concept of poverty concerns a different order of need, one not accessible through the effort to know the physical requirements of the organism conceived as a natural creature.

Notions of poverty derive from notions of living, and take their significance from the significance we invest in the idea of living a life of a certain kind. Because of this, solving the problem of physical survival does not solve the problem of poverty. We may survive physically while losing the meaning that life has had, or is meant to have, for us. When this happens, we are still poor, though our basic needs may be satisfied. Yet, such a life is hardly worth living and, because of this, when restricted to it, we remain poor.

To say that such a life is hardly worth living introduces a judgment we cannot derive from objectively defined attributes of the species. Rather, making such a judgment requires that we link our conception of need and poverty to norms. In other words, it makes our thinking about poverty part of our thinking about the ethical standing of institutions and ways of life. It is important that we make clear from the outset that a conception of poverty depends in this way on an ideal of living rather than on a purely positive description of life as it is.

---

[1] We use the term "prescriptive" to refer to needs that are given from the outset and to a theory of poverty based on this conception of needs. Some use the same term more broadly to mean normative. We use it here in the more restricted sense that we indicate.

Following this line of thought might encourage appeal to something like the cultural subsistence emphasized by the classical economists. Here, survival takes on the added significance of cultural survival. Poverty means loss of connection to the community, of position in the community, or of investment of meaning in the ways of life defined by the community. Community here refers not simply to an aggregation of persons, or a system of interdependence in need satisfaction, but to a set of ways of life appropriate to group membership and shared group identity. Dominance within it of shared group identities linked to assigned positions in a social structure enable the community to have prior knowledge of what its members need if they are to be a part of the community, which is their subsistence.

The approach just briefly summarized, because it depends so heavily on group membership and group identity, poses problems in contexts where the hold of the group over the member is for some reason weakened, as tends to be the case in modern societies. These problems come from two interconnected sources. The first has to do with the presence of more than one community, more than one culture. Here, no single definition of subsistence and therefore of poverty can be applied. A subsistence that secures well-being according to one community's standards might mean impoverishment by another community's standards. This means that inequality of provision must be the rule so far as the implementation of poverty policy is concerned. This inequality of provision tends to undermine the moral authority of the ideal expressed in provision for the poor when members of different cultural communities must live together. But, more than this, it also suggests a deeper challenge to the moral authority of the subsistence. Differences between communities mean differences in values that express the group's underlying moral judgments. These differences undermine any claim to universality of moral judgment, which in turn undermines the moral authority of the ways of life defined for the group members. We discuss the matter of universality further at the end of Chapter 4.

The issue of inequality has a larger significance for the problem of cultural subsistence. So far, we have assumed that if members of a community have access to their subsistence they are not poor. But, this may not be the case. When the community is structured around a strong norm of inequality, and when that norm defines some members as fully persons and others as less than persons, the subsistence of the latter still leaves them impoverished in an important sense of the term. They still lack something vital in living.

When this is true, the idea of the cultural subsistence as the basis for determining poverty shares a defect we identified with the idea of basic need: you may have your cultural subsistence and still be poor, an idea Marx takes up in his critique of political economy when he insists that we consider impoverishment a relative matter. When inequality is the basis for social cohesion, poverty is built into culture and community norms. This means that access to subsistence cannot determine who is or is not poor. Rather, it is rank in society that establishes this division.

The idea of subsistence in the classical economists, its heritage in medieval thinking, its relation to policies with continuing relevance such as the English poor laws, and its connection with labor markets, are important in thinking about poverty, and we discuss them in detail in Chapter 2. The relation of subsistence to medieval thinking can be seen in the concept of a moral order, and the associated idea that economic life should express and embody a spiritual end. In a moral order, we find a system of rights and obligations in which the member is made subordinate to the needs of the larger collective unit. Subsistence, in this setting, carries moral authority since individuals must receive what is their due.

The attempt to define poverty on the basis of the norms appropriate to a moral order runs into difficulty when we move to a modern rather than subsistence-based economy. In a modern economy there is a shift in the basis of normative judgment from the sustenance of the community to securing the rights of the individual (Chapter 5). Unlike the moral order, a modern economy finds its normative basis in the idea of freedom and especially individual self-determination. This shift in the basis for normative judgment requires a shift in the conception of poverty, and in the policies through which the problem of poverty is addressed. We can no longer take the idea of subsistence for granted, and assume it is well defined in the way it might be in a moral order. This means that we need to think about poverty in a different way, one that is consistent with the norm of individual self-determination, and therefore includes the opportunity to live a life that is not wholly, or even essentially, determined by ascribed group identity. Autonomy does not make the individual indifferent to group affiliation, but it does undermine the authority of the group over his or her way of life, and in so doing calls into question the authority of the ideal of cultural subsistence that can only be well defined in relation to a given culture and community. It is this norm of freedom or autonomy that forces us to look beyond the subsistence and the moral order in which it is sometimes defined for our understanding of what it means to be poor and of what can and should be done about it.

Despite the difficulty in reconciling prescriptive theory with a normative order organized around the ideal of individual autonomy, the idea that we can somehow identify a set of goods whose consumption is adequate to sustain human life, and use the availability or lack of those goods to determine who is or who is not poor continues to have a powerful hold on thinking about poverty. Conventional methods for specifying the poverty line run into difficulty because they attempt to apply elements of the traditional idea of subsistence in a setting where no such notion applies, as we discuss in detail in Chapter 3.

The method for measuring poverty used by the United States government, first introduced by Molly Orshansky of the Social Security administration in the 1960s, offers a good example of this.[2] Orshansky based her definition of the poverty level on the cheapest of a set of food plans developed by dieticians at the Department of Agriculture, specifically that food plan designed for temporary use during emergencies. The cost of the food plan was then adjusted to produce an overall poverty level by assuming that expenditures on food accounted for about a third of normal family expenses. So, the poverty level was defined as the cost of the emergency food plan multiplied by three.

This way of thinking about poverty incorporates one important aspect of the idea of subsistence while dropping another. It defines a level of living independent of the individual, individual identity, and self-chosen modes of living, in favor of a universal standard of consumption ostensibly linked to physical need. Because of its independence from the individual, this measure can be considered a version of the idea of subsistence. Yet, the definition of the poverty level differs from the older idea of subsistence in leaving aside the element that ties subsistence to the needs of a specific cultural and social order and thus makes subsistence contingent and variable. The failure of efforts to adapt the poverty measure defined in the 1960s to changes in overall living standards, which would acknowledge that the subsistence is that of a social and moral creature, reinforces the idea that the poverty line should be defined without considering elements vital to the traditional notion of subsistence (Fisher 1997).

By leaving aside the moral element in the subsistence, the current convention attempts to define subsistence outside the moral order. This is natural enough in a context where the moral order does not exist, or at least is not compelling. When we seek to determine subsistence outside a moral order, we inevitably end up with the sort of quasi-physiological determination of need favored in the US government's calculation. The result is not, in the end, very convincing on any normative grounds, and does not express any meaningful notion of poverty or

---

[2] The following summary is taken from Fisher (1997).

offer any meaningful answer to the question: What do the poor lack that makes them poor?

The conventional approach to setting the poverty level expresses, among other factors, the difficulty in a modern society of determining subsistence. A similar problem is seen in the attempt to apply the notion of basic needs in development economics (see Chapter 4). This problem arises when modes of life are not prescribed for the individual and fixed according to tradition, but are malleable according to individual differences and the process of social change driven by the power of individual difference. Where we have ranks in society that either do not change at all, or change only very slowly, we can define the subsistence according to the ways of life and corresponding needs defined within those ranks. Outside of this context, the ideas of subsistence and of a poverty line determined by failure to acquire the subsistence have nothing to grab onto. Since the definition of the poverty line attempts to use a subsistence-like calculation where no such calculation is possible, it inevitably appears arbitrary.

Not only is the resulting definition of poverty arbitrary, however. It is also, at least implicitly, punitive. A punitive element is implied when we treat those who are poor as creatures not only outside a moral order, since their sustenance has no moral determination, but also outside the order of individual property owners and citizens, since their subsistence does not sustain them as individuals. The punitive element results where no cultural floor is recognized, and those setting the poverty line are thus free to push it toward a bare physical limit, depriving the poor of their connection to a cultural or social norm.

The punitive element in poverty policy, in both its older and contemporary forms, is closely linked to the importance of Puritan ideas (see Chapter 2). For the Puritan, salvation was an individual matter, and worth in the eyes of God depended on the individual will. Failures, such as those leading to poverty, consequently were failures of will. In this way of thinking, responsibility for poverty rested with the character of the poor and not the circumstances in which they found themselves. It is around these two poles, character and circumstance, that poverty policies tend to cluster (see Chapter 3).

In his survey of ideas about poverty, T. H. Marshall suggests that we organize our thinking around pairs of related concepts (Marshall 1981: 40–45). Among these pairs are dependency – want and absolute – relative. Subsistence-based theories tend to conceive poverty not in terms of dependence, but in terms of want. They also pose the question of poverty in absolute terms, as the inability to lead a well-defined way of life, which is, roughly speaking, something we either can or cannot do given our resources. The defects in the subsistence-based theory briefly mentioned above are connected to the fact that they define poverty on the basis of need and in absolute terms, which might encourage us to move to the opposing poles indicated above, and either consider poverty a matter of dependence or conceive it in relative rather than absolute terms.

A relative definition of poverty simply measures the standard of living available to the individual against "the current level of civilization in the country concerned," which is, in turn, "represented by the average" of existing levels of income (Marshall 1981: 43). By opting for a relative definition of poverty, we would sidestep the difficulties we have in identifying a specific set of needs and predetermined way of life in a context where the moral authority of the community has weakened. This makes relative concepts of poverty appealing in a world where governing norms center on individual self-determination.

It is, of course, hard to say in what way an average such as that used to calculate relative impoverishment carries any moral authority, since it is really nothing more than a statistical artifact. Clearly, in a society where a strong norm of equality prevailed, such an average would have meaning; but at the same time it would not help us to define poverty since the variance around the mean would be small, and therefore poverty by the relative definition would be non-existent. To make sense of the notion of relative poverty, it might be more helpful to speak not in terms of the average, but in terms of a more general notion of the "current level of civilization," treating that as a proxy for the older idea of a cultural and historical subsistence. Yet, outside the average, the current level of civilization will only have meaning so far as there exists a significant degree of equality among citizens. In the context of a significant degree of inequality, it is hard to see what the current level of civilization could mean. The problem is, of course, compounded in a multicultural society. All of this suggests that the relative notion of poverty, as appealing as it might be as a solution to the problem created by the failure of the subsistence idea, does not really lead us to a meaningful and compelling idea of what it means to be poor, and especially what it is that we lack when we are poor.

The idea that being poor means being dependent does take us in a direction different from that mapped out by the idea of subsistence, without requiring that we appeal to the sort of arbitrary considerations brought into play by the idea that we calculate the poverty line in relation to an average level of income. If we consider, specifically, dependence on a public authority, there is, of course, the risk that using this definition will make our concept of poverty derive from contingent policies of government. Yet, the idea that poverty is a state of dependence remains important, the problem being how we can conceive dependence and therefore independence so they can shape policy rather than being defined by it. If being poor means being dependent, then what the poor lack is the capacity to live autonomously. To understand what it means to be poor means to understand what it means to be independent, and why some are not.

We think it clear enough that if we are to develop a meaningful concept of poverty we must look somewhere other than the subsistence. This means considering a non-prescriptive theory of poverty, which begins with a non-prescriptive theory of need. We cannot assume from the outset that we know what individuals need. If our thinking about poverty is part of a larger understanding of the institutions and policies through which the ideal of individual self-determination can be realized, then our thinking about poverty cannot begin with an attempt to prescribe needs for the individual since doing so would violate the norm of self-determination. This is appropriate to thinking about an autonomous person, one not predetermined by nature or social position. We try to develop a meaningful concept of poverty that does not center on specifying of a set of needs that, when left unmet, imply that we are poor.

An important step in this direction has been taken by Martha Nussbaum and Amartya Sen with the suggestion that subsistence-related ideas be replaced with the idea of human capabilities, a development we address in Chapter 4. The idea of human capabilities may or may not lead us toward a non-prescriptive theory of poverty depending on how we understand the nature and origin of the capabilities. So far as we simply replace a list of needs with a list of capabilities, a crucial element of the prescriptive approach reappears in the capabilities idea. However, this may not be inevitable, depending on how we understand capabilities and, more specifically, how we understand capabilities in relation to freedom. Sen's suggestion that we consider capabilities in relation to freedom would tend to move the capabilities idea in a direction more conducive to a non-prescriptive theory of poverty. What is needed to pin down a conception of poverty as capabilities deprivation appropriate to a non-prescriptive theory is a closer specification of what Sen and Nussbaum might refer to as the beings and doings appropriate to an individual living in a society organized around a norm of freedom. Focusing on the doings appropriate in such a setting requires paying special attention to the kind of work suitable to a free person, and to those factors that might impede individuals from finding and doing such work.

In specifying the kind of work appropriate to a free person, we will emphasize the idea of creativity as it has been formulated by Donald Winnicott in his work on early emotional development (see Chapter 6). We attempt to integrate Winnicott's notion of creativity and of creative living with the capabilities idea as formulated by Nussbaum and Sen. We will define poverty as the inability to do the creative work appropriate to living the life of a free person. Creativity in work is considered the exercise of a human capability connected to skilled labor (see Chapter 7). Poverty results either when this capability does not develop, or when the opportunity to exercise it is unavailable. In this conception, the problem of poverty involves the need to facilitate the development of specific capabilities, and then to secure an environment in which those capabilities can be exercised as far as that is possible.

An objection may arise to our emphasis on skilled work as the doing that is appropriate to free human beings in a modern setting. The classical and neoclassical economists both saw work as opposed to freedom. Adam Smith and Karl Marx wrote of repetitive and boring work, and of the activity of workers being closer to that of machines than that of humans. The neoclassical conception of work opposes it to satisfaction, seeing freedom from work as enhancing satisfaction and work taking away from it. Work, in both of these conceptions, is something to be avoided. While we agree that work may have undesirable qualities, we stress that this is not necessary. It seems reasonable to assume that machine-like, unskilled work is associated primarily with an earlier phase of capitalist development, and that current trends enhance the availability of skilled work sufficiently to justify our beginning to treat it as a norm. Moreover, the evidence from surveys indicates that work of the kind we emphasize provides an intrinsic satisfaction. These matters are discussed in Chapter 8.

Winnicott suggests that the capacity for creativity and creative living is an achievement requiring a specific development and an appropriate, or "facilitating," environment. This means that not all individuals will be able to make use of this capacity. It is likely, then, that there are those who will be unable to make work the exercise of creativity through the use of skill. They will instead experience work as something simply to be endured for the sake of pay (see Chapter 9). Those who experience work in this way, even when work of the appropriate kind is available, lack something vital in living and are, in this sense, poor.

If we use the term development to refer to the process of acquiring relevant capabilities, then eliminating poverty is simply the other side of development, and cannot be accomplished without it (see Chapter 10). This is not primarily because development increases the resources available to satisfy needs, but because development means putting in place the institutions needed to facilitate the process of acquiring the requisite capability or capabilities. Poverty policy is, then, development policy, and we cannot expect to remove poverty if we cannot foster a successful process of economic, social, and individual development.

In developing a non-prescriptive theory of poverty, we are aware that we speak only indirectly and partially to what is normally assumed to be the problem of poverty: low living standards, poor housing, inadequate health care, and so on. This is inevitable in a treatment of poverty that does not center attention on matters of living standards, but on norms underlying ways of life, and normatively valued capabilities to lead a life of a particular kind. The idea of poverty as the inability to live creatively does not correspond very precisely to the idea that poverty is about living standards, but the two may still be connected. Indeed, we will argue that they are closely linked. But, they are not the same thing. Someone may be poor by our definition whose living standard does not seem inadequate by the arbitrary, yet in some ways compelling, standard of a deviation from the mean level of living in society.

Given the non-prescriptive standard developed here, we can distinguish between policy that seeks, at least in some measure, to change the factors that underlie poverty, and policy that seeks to ameliorate the effects of poverty on the quality of life of the poor without changing the underlying factors responsible for poverty. Policy of this second kind is important, indeed vitally so, whether or not it addresses the factors causing poverty. Imagining what sort of policy will significantly reduce the incidence of poverty is a much more difficult matter, however. As we pursue our discussion of poverty and work, we keep this distinction in mind.

In thinking about poverty policy, another matter should be addressed. Given the importance we place on individual self-determination, it may be thought that there is no place for concern for others as a driving force toward policy that might alleviate poverty. We address this issue in Chapter 10, where we consider how a society organized around a norm of individual autonomy and creative living might incorporate regard for others, which is necessary if there is to be any real concern for dealing with the problem of poverty.

*Part I*

# 2 The classical period

Around the time economics as a coherent body of thought was emerging, there was a change in the perception of the poor. This came near the end of a long development. R. H. Tawney describes this change as a shift between the medieval "conception of society as a community of unequal classes with varying functions, organized for a common end" and the modern idea of society "as a mechanism adjusting through the play of economic motives to the supply of economic needs" (1962: 13).

It is possible to argue against the simplicity of Tawney's picture. The chasm may not have been as wide as he imagined or its beginning and ending points located exactly as he stated. Nevertheless, as Gertrude Himmelfarb suggests, to deny the gap "entirely is, in a sense to affirm it." The claim that society is and always was nothing more than the sum of the strivings of individuals in the material world, that the economy is and was independent from and never subjugated to other motives and standards, is a "peculiarly modern way of thinking, patently at variance with the beliefs most people lived with for most of history" (Himmelfarb 1983: 23–24).

Tawney found the origin of this change in thinking in the sixteenth century with the spread of commercial agriculture. It continued and hastened with the spread of industrial activity after that time. He located the new ethic in the teachings of Puritanism, which diverged sharply in many respects from medieval beliefs. In the medieval view:

Peasant and lord, in their different degrees, are members of one Christian commonwealth, within which the law of charity must bridle the corroding appetite for economic gain. In such a mystical corporation, knit together by mutual obligations, no man may press his advantage to the full, for no man may seek to live "outside the body of the Church." (Tawney 1962: 255)

In this conception of mutual obligation, rich and poor formed a "spiritual economy of salvation." The pauper waited for "others to discharge their duty toward him; this gave him a claim upon others, in exchange for which he incurred the obligation to pray for their souls."

Otherwise, given the lesson of the fable comparing the difficulty of a rich man entering heaven to that of a camel passing through eye of a needle, the rich would not achieve salvation. Because of this system, the poor were seen to be an important part of society, and they collectively achieved a social standing that they were to lose in later years.

> The poor, or at any rate a particular class of the poor, were afforded a place in society, a place both in the natural economy of the world and the spiritual economy of salvation . . . In virtue of their function, a place, although an admittedly inferior one, was found in the social hierarchy for laborers and artisans. (Mollat 1986: 105)

In the logic of medieval times, to be part of society was to have a function in it. The poor had an important function in promoting salvation so that, however miserable was their existence, they were part of society and not marginal to it (Mollat 1986: 105–107). It is easy, then, to agree with Geremek's claim that in medieval times:

> the most important factors in determining ideological attitudes towards poverty, and to a great extent also the social status of the poor, are to be found in the sphere of the sacred, a fundamental source of differences in the medieval and modern approaches to the problems of poverty. (Geremek 1994: 7)

The change emphasized by Tawney can be seen in the altered religious attitude of the Puritans. For them, the medieval economy of salvation made no sense. Instead, the revelation of God to the individual became the centerpiece of Puritan theology, "dismissing as dross and vanity all else but this secret and solitary communion" (Tawney 1962: 226). Salvation is made the direct gift of God, "unmediated by any earthly institution." Life was a personal struggle, which was fought by a relentless dedication to work. Obstacles, such as the temptation to be extravagant with the fruits of work, were tests of spiritual value. Given that the work was the task of a divine "calling," failure to succeed at it was a spiritual defect. Yet success, while it meant that the Puritan was following the right path, was no reason to slacken. This mindset accorded well with an emphasis on production at an ever-increasing scale, the novel idea of "economic progress as an end to be consciously sought, while ever receding" (Tawney 1962: 249). Sufficiency to the needs of traditional, largely static, relationships was replaced by a focus on increase and expansion. The medieval assessment of poverty as valuable to society – since it was valuable to spiritual life – was lost.

The ethic of Puritanism had other consequences for thinking about poverty. The Puritan ideals of individual responsibility and achievement express a single conviction about the individual: that action depends on will. According to Tawney, the essence of Puritanism is will, "will organized and disciplined and inspired . . . quiescent in rapt adoration or straining in violent energy. . ." (1962: 201). The idea of will summarized a whole conception of the individual. In this conception, emphasis shifts from the individual's embeddedness in society to the individual's inner life and separate being. The deployment of the concept of will, and the associated isolation of the individual's relation with God, implied moral self-sufficiency. The Puritan's moral self-sufficiency "nerved his will, but . . . corroded his sense of social solidarity. For, if each individual's destiny hangs on a private transaction between himself and his maker, what room is left for human intervention?" (Tawney 1962: 227–228).

This conception of the human condition leaves little room for any attitude toward those who fail that does not interpret their failure as of their own making, and thus as resulting from inner flaws, for "character is all and circumstances nothing" (Tawney 1962: 230). As Max Weber points out, sympathy for the downtrodden was driven out by "hatred and contempt" (1958: 122). Tawney goes on to suggest that it is a small step from the idea of individual responsibility to dismantling those protections for the poor that express social obligation. Where individual will and responsibility are all, social obligation can mean very little. The older doctrines of riches detracting from spiritual worth,[1] or of poverty as something to emulate (as medieval monks would do), were consequently replaced, though this alteration was a long and not always even process.

### Mercantilism and the Old Poor Law

If poverty is a matter of character, then the solution to it, if there is one, has to do either with devising a social mechanism that can produce something of worth despite character being what it is, or in reforming character. Both of these approaches were used by the mercantilists in the seventeenth century to advance the interests of the state and in the contemporary enactments of policy toward the poor.[2] These developments are best understood by referring to the mercantilist conception of what advanced state interest.

The medieval image of society as a body and its members as parts was adapted to describe the nation. Hobbes's *Leviathan* begins with the image of "that great Leviathan, called Commonwealth, or State (in

---

[1] Now, on the contrary, the Puritan saw in "riches, not an object of suspicion . . . but the blessing which rewards the triumph of energy and will" (Tawney, 1962: 230).

[2] The idea that poverty is a personal failure is of great consequence to current thinking also and is explored more fully in Chapter 3. The exposition in this section relies on Dean (1991).

Latin, Civitas), which is but an artificial man." The parts of a body have no independent being. Thus Hobbes calls civil war death for the body. This image resonated well with the group of writers known as mercantilists, given their focus on the nation, to whose welfare all else is subordinated. One of them, reflecting a very common view, wrote, "The poorer sort . . . are the hands and feet, the wealth and strength of the nation" (cited in Furniss (1920: 22n) along with many other examples).

For mercantilists, the welfare of the nation is not the sum of the welfare of its individual members; rather, the welfare of the nation is what determines what its members ought to do and to be. In this sense, the functionalistic attitude with respect to the poor – that they had a role to play – was a connection to medieval thought that the mercantilists maintained.

But mercantilist and medieval thinkers differed in the goals that they thought society should pursue. For mercantilists, the goal was to increase the wealth and power of the nation rather than to promote a direct spiritual purpose. As the scope of economic activity extended to become truly national and international, it was no longer guided by local imperatives. Instead, the statesman became the guide of the national economy. This differs from the later, classical view that the economy needs no guide since it is self-regulating: the invisible hand replaces the visible one (Levine 2001: 139). For mercantilists, then, the role of the poor was to promote the nation's wealth. The thought was as follows: a nation's wealth derived from foreign trade, success in which arose from the ability to sell cheaply; the ability to do so in turn depended on a large population and low wages (Furniss 1950: 30–31). Thus poverty and national wealth were consistent with one another. This led to a divergence between the meaning attached to "poverty" and "the poor." Poverty referred to the fortune of the nation as a whole and was consistent with the poor being impoverished. Thus Petty could write, "Fewness of people is real poverty" (Petty 1963: 34).

"The poor" meant laborers, broadly conceived. They were poor because their only livelihood was recourse to farming or manufacturing work. The rough equation of the number of laborers and national wealth was refined so that the poor comprised three categories, as Dean (1991) relates. In the formula of a seventeenth-century author relating obligations to the poor, there should be: "work for those that will labour, punishment for those that will not, and bread for those that cannot" (cited in Eden 1928: 36). This division encompasses the able pauper who is willing and able to work, the idle poor treated as rogues and vagabonds, and the sick and infirm who are simply unable to work. In the mercantilist desire to increase the nation's wealth, a key goal was to find work for those who would labor and to find means of disciplining those who were idle to get them to labor. By these means, unproductive labor would be converted to productive labor, and national wealth would increase.

The means for accomplishing this was what came to be known as the Old Poor Law. Enacted around 1600 and revised many times, the Old Poor Law had a number of provisions. Those able to work were to be given a wage in return for work, or they were given "outdoor" relief, a stipend outside of a workhouse. The idle poor were to be punished so that they could learn the error of their ways. Those who were old or infirm were to be kept in almshouses or hospitals. The laws were administered at the level of the parish, a small unit, of which there were about 50,000 in England. They were financed by compulsory taxes on property owners. The Old Poor Law, being administered locally, varied significantly in its application (Webb and Webb 1963).

The issue of character surfaces strongly here. Leaving aside the third category of the poor, those who simply are unable to work, the issue becomes whether a poor person will work. If not, the solution of the Old Poor Law is punishment. This continues and codifies into law a view that the mere fact of poverty signifies crime or sin. Like sinners, the poor are beyond the pale of decent society, and are therefore to be feared and punished.

Problems with the Old Poor Law became evident over time.[3] Migration in search of jobs or of better benefits threatened to swamp certain parishes with obligations to the poor. The Act of Settlement was passed stating that poor relief was to be granted only to those born in the parish or those who had passed other stringent requirements.[4]

The migration of labor within a national labor market mirrors the shift from local to national authority: the centralization of legal authority and military power within the boundaries of the nation-state, as argued for by Hobbes. This involved the dissolution of local privileges and autonomous jurisdictions within the state. At the same time, it meant that, increasingly, workers were neither constrained nor protected by local authorities. As this transformation took place, people who were tied to localities because of hierarchical relations with a master, now became "masterless men" (Beier 1985). Eventually, a class of workers, untied to specific locales was created. In other words, there came into being a

---

[3] The Old Poor Law remained in effect until the passage of the New Poor Law of 1834.
[4] Adam Smith later criticized the Act of Settlement provisions in particular since they impeded the mobility of labor: workers were forced to stay where they were born rather than go where there were jobs (Smith 1937: 135–142).

modern labor market. A myriad of historical events comprised this transformation (Polanyi 1957b: ch. 6). From these developments, workers came to be available as labor for capitalist enterprise and could be seen as members of a class. Thus, understanding poverty increasingly became a matter of understanding labor. The classical economists including Marx took important steps in this direction.[5]

### Labor and subsistence

In thinking about a general labor market, the classical thinkers developed their ideas in contrast to the medieval and premodern notion of the particularity of work. One way to see this contrast is to consider the issue of value arising in exchange. Aristotle, for example, wrote very much in a premodern vein that:

The number of shoes exchanged for a house (or for a given amount of food) must therefore correspond to the ratio of builder to shoemaker or if this be not so, there will be no exchange and no intercourse . . . There will, then, be reciprocity when the terms have been equated so that as farmer is to shoemaker, the amount of the shoemaker's work is to that of the farmer's work for which it exchanges. (Aristotle 1984: V.5)

While Aristotle speaks of the need for commensurability if exchange is to take place, he does not identify what is common to things traded. Thus he does not identify labor as such, measured in hours, as that which brings regularity to exchanges. Instead, labor seems to be identified with its particular place in the moral order and is itself particular. So in this premodern context, price is governed by the cost of "what was necessary to maintain the producer" (Roll 1953: 46). This leads to the notion of just price, which was followed in the medieval period as well. In the context of society as a whole, "just terms of exchange must be such as ensure that the different arts subsist to produce what society needs" (Langholm 1979: 35).

Marx interpreted the problem that Aristotle faced as follows. Aristotle was unable to arrive at what was common among commodities; unable to derive a theory of value, "because Greek society was founded on the labour of slaves, hence had as its natural basis the inequality of men and of their labour-powers." Given the status hierarchies of precapitalist societies, there was no commensurability of labor and it could not serve as a common measure. Yet for the classical economists, this is just what was common in commodities – "human labour in general" – but this

---

[5] In this discussion, we group Marx with the classical economists.

"could not be deciphered until the concept of human equality had already acquired the permanence of a fixed popular opinion" (Marx 1977a: 152). Following on Marx's critique of Aristotle, we can say that the classical economists thought of workers as having a kind of equality that was inconceivable in the medieval period. There was a leveling of workers that contrasts with the hierarchical organization of earlier societies.

Adam Smith related the development by which workers arrived at this point to the tendency in capitalist enterprise toward an ever-greater division of labor. This would seem to move in the direction of less equality rather than greater since, as Smith says, the division of labor creates "an almost infinite variety" of occupations in society. But this is to forget an important contrast. Workers in a medieval, craft-based system were not interchangeable, given that skills were not transferable. In the capitalist division of labor that Smith anticipated, however, labor consisted of simple, repetitive tasks that could be done by almost anyone. Thus in a premodern setting, the division of labor is an expression of social differentiation, whereas in the classical setting, the division of labor eliminates the need for separate and specific skills. The less emphasis there is on skills, the more likely it is that workers are interchangeable, and the sort of equality that Marx saw missing in Aristotle emerges. Thus it is easier to conceive of labor in general, dissociated from the particularities found in skilled work. From this we might say that there are really two divisions of labor. One is based on differences arising from skilled trades. The other is the newer idea based on the loss of skills, the subdivision and disintegration of productive tasks, and the associated homogenization of labor tasks. In the first, it matters who is doing what job. In the second, the jobs differ, but who is doing them is not important. In this sense, there are no intrinsic differences among workers.

The equality of workers posited by the classical economists has an important consequence for thinking about poverty. It means that the classical economists could consistently apply the notion of subsistence to determining the wage. Since workers were seen as homogeneous in function, they could receive a uniform subsistence. The classical economists all held that we could state what workers require at a given point in the development of a society. With variation in norms and changing customs, the requirements of workers, their subsistence needs, will also change. Thus the classical notion of subsistence is, on the whole, not a biological notion (for details, see Levine 1998: ch. 1). In Adam Smith's formulation, it includes not only the necessities but also the conveniences of life. Custom tells us what the worker, as a functioning member of society, requires. Subsistence thus denotes the role of the worker in society.

In an important sense, there is substantial continuity between the medieval and classical conceptions. In both, the concept of subsistence signifies what workers expect and are owed by society in order to maintain a particular way of life and to perform their functions. There are also contrasts. The medieval economy was governed by a higher moral purpose and so constituted a moral order.[6] The economy conceived by the classical economists no longer embodies a higher spiritual purpose, but maintains the system of rights and obligations that go along with subsistence. The relations between workers and their setting differ, however. In the premodern world, there is close interaction between workers and their masters, often life-long relations, rather than a changing labor market; workers are seen to have differences in skill and ability, rather than being interchangeable; and there is little mobility for workers rather than a national labor market. In both conceptions, though, for a worker not to receive subsistence meant poverty since it meant not receiving what was sufficient for a person to maintain a particular way of life or position in society.

### Poverty and the logic of capitalism

While for the classical economists a lack of subsistence was sufficient to signify poverty, it was not necessary. It is now possible for workers to be poor – in other words, poverty does not result only from lack of work.[7] As national labor markets grew, "workers were assimilated to the poor" (Geremek 1994: 233). Since workers were essential to capitalism, this thought raised the issue of the connection between capitalism

---

[6] The phrase "moral order" was used by Marx to describe the structure of older societies. The phrase appears in his discussion of the power of money to corrode such an order. Money "extinguishes all distinctions . . . Ancient society therefore denounced it as tending to destroy the moral order" (1977a: 229–230). Other authors, for example, Polanyi, similarly contrasted the structure of traditional and modern economies: "Broadly, the proposition holds that all economic systems known to us up to the end of feudalism in Western Europe were organized . . . [so that] the orderly production and distribution of goods was secured through a great variety of individual motives disciplined by general principles of behavior. Among these motives gain was not prominent. Custom and law, magic and religion co-operated in inducing the individual to comply with rules of behavior which, eventually, ensured his functioning in the economic system" (Polanyi 1957b: 54–55).

[7] If poverty can arise even if the worker receives subsistence, poverty needs to be defined without reference to subsistence. The classical economists' approach to this issue, having to do with the character of work, is discussed later in this section. The discussion of Townsend and Mandeville below relies on Dean (1991), who also provides the quotations from them.

and poverty. Further, since workers could be poor and a mass labor market was created, poverty could emerge on a large scale. Thus:

> Poverty as a mass phenomenon, however, did not appear until the medieval world was already giving way to a new era; this is why the transition from feudal to capitalist society and from agrarian to industrial structures was such an important period for economic history and the sociology of pauperization. (Geremek 1994: 11)

The classical economists considered this conjunction of the advent of capitalism and the phenomenon of mass poverty. The idea that poverty is part of capitalism "is quite distinct from the medieval theory according to which the poor had a necessary place in the system of distribution of tasks and functions in Christian society" (Geremek 1994: 231). Nevertheless, a form of continuity can be seen as well. In both settings, poverty results from the functioning of society. Previously, the genesis of poverty is the sacred realm as reflected in the structure of society; in the classical view, the connection results because of the working of the economy, now seen as an autonomous entity with its own laws. To understand the poor, then, becomes a task of figuring out their place within the economic system, to see poverty as a "mass phenomenon." For Marx, the history of capitalism in England showed that the accumulation of capital was built on the basis of poverty for the mass of people (Marx 1977a: 876).

In addition to Marx's large claim that the genesis of capitalism involved the creation of poverty, and that its progress exacerbated it, there was the related though smaller claim that poverty encouraged a reliable supply of labor. Before Marx, Townsend ([1786]1971) saw poverty's concomitant hunger "exerting a gentle, silent but relentless pressure" that also inclined "people to great effort, for it is the most natural motive for work." Similarly, Mandeville (1714/1924) held that without the needs that went unsatisfied with poverty, "no one would work," adding that "in a free nation, where slavery is forbidden, the surest treasure is the existence of large numbers of working poor."

While poverty was seen as necessary to economic functioning, it could also run amok. The work of Malthus, discussed below, with its emphasis on population growth running up against meager subsistence, is an indication of this line of thinking. If workers were poor, it was not because they lacked subsistence. From this we see the beginnings of the distinction between poverty and lack of subsistence, which means that the idea of subsistence is not the key to the idea of poverty. One could argue that poverty meant simply that workers had too few of the things that made up subsistence (on this idea, see Chapter 4). But Smith and Marx arrived at a different conclusion. For them, it was the nature of work that led to serious dissatisfaction and to a reduction in workers' welfare. In this sense, workers would be poor – not for lack of subsistence or material goods – even if they were working and were able to acquire subsistence. Smith spoke of the degradation of moral and intellectual virtues consequent on doing repetitive, machine-like work.

> In the progress of the division of labour, the employment of the far greater part of those who live by labour . . . comes to be confined to a few very simple operations, frequently one or two . . . The man whose whole life is spent in performing a few simple operations, of which the effects too are, perhaps, always the same, or very nearly the same, has no occasion to exert his understanding, or to exercise his invention in finding out expedients for removing difficulties which never occur. He naturally loses, therefore the habit of such exertion . . . His dexterity at his own particular trade seems, in this manner, to be acquired at the expense of his intellectual, social and martial virtues. (Smith 1937: 734–735)

It seems to be this sort of labor that Smith had in mind when he wrote that by laboring a worker lays down a "portion of his ease, his liberty, and his happiness" (Smith 1937: 33). In other words, not only is this sort of laboring injurious in its subsequent effects, but it also is deadening more immediately, in its very doing. Workers in such a state are hardly well-off and might reasonably be called poor even though they do not lack subsistence.

Smith's vision in these passages is quite dark. He calls this view of labor characteristic of civilized society, contrasting it with the well-rounded work of previous societies. So far as work under capitalism was concerned, Marx too emphasized the negative aspects of work, its harmfulness to workers, a harmfulness he formulated in the language of alienation. In his view, workers are alienated in two senses. First, they no longer have a connection to the product of their work, which is now the property of the capitalist. Second, they are also alienated from the process of work, which is now controlled by the capitalist. "The alienation of the object of labor merely summarizes the alienation in the work activity itself" (Marx 1964: 124). With this separation of the worker's personality from the process and outcome of work, work becomes foreign to the worker's sense of self. "Work is *external* to the worker . . . It is not part of his nature; consequently he does not fulfill himself in his work but denies himself . . . The worker therefore feels himself at home only during his leisure time, whereas at work he feels homeless" (Marx 1964: 124–125).[8] Thus far, Marx's views are consistent with Smith's.

---

[8] As in the neoclassical setting, albeit for different reasons, work becomes something that must be endured and leisure becomes the contrasting activity that has positive connotations.

Yet, Marx indicated another possibility for the relation of work to the worker. He dissociated "attractive work, the individual's self-realisation" from two other visions: first, Smith's idea that work inevitably becomes degraded, and second, Fourier's desire for work to become mere fun and amusement. (These are in essence the two poles we see in the later, neoclassical framework: work as disutility and pseudo-work such as volunteering, which is really leisure, as utility.) Instead, Marx argues that work can be engaging and free while at the same time being challenging, serious, and taxing. So, in such work, "the overcoming of obstacles is in itself a liberating activity . . . Really free working, e.g., composing, is at the same time precisely the most damned seriousness, the most intense exertion" (Marx 1973: 611). In this new setting, the opposition of labor and leisure is confounded since labor does not have to be regarded purely as sacrifice (of leisure) if the "worker should, e.g., enjoy his work" (Marx 1973: 612). While Marx's discussion suggests that work may have a more wholesome relation to workers' welfare, his analysis of capitalism suggests that this sort of work cannot be found in capitalist economies.[9]

### Classical political economy and the New Poor Law

The classical economists treated the economy as a system and attempted to discern the tendencies by which it would evolve. They attempted to uncover its "law of motion," in Marx's phrase, rather than focus on the "political arithmetic" of the mercantilists. They attempted to apply this way of thinking to the question of poor relief. In doing so, Smith developed two propositions that were taken up by the other classical economists. First, he treated labor in economic terms:

The demand for men, like that for every commodity necessarily regulates the production of men, quicken when it goes too slowly, and stops when it advances too fast. (Smith 1937: 80)

Second, he identified limits to growth and the tendency for wages to be driven down to the subsistence level:

In a country fully peopled in proportion to either what its territory could maintain or its stock employ, the competition for employment would necessarily be so great as to reduce the wages of labour to what was barely sufficient to keep up the number of labourers, and the country being fully peopled, that number could never be augmented. (Smith 1937: 94–95)

---

[9] Our own view is that this conclusion is too pessimistic (see Chapter 8). Marx's conclusion might well apply to the establishment phases of capitalism, but does not seem to hold, at least fully, in more recent times.

Consequently, the "most distinctive feature" of the classical growth theory is to see growth leading inexorably toward a stationary state (Deane 1978: 37).

The development of a labor market meant that an impersonal mechanism rather than the personal relations of the premodern set-up was seen to determine wages. More and more, outcomes for workers seemed to devolve into matters of individual initiative and the functioning of the marketplace, rather than matters of public responsibility. Partly this was because the economy was seen as having its own inexorable movement. Thus there was a shift from the traditional notion of a right to subsistence, which prevailed for workers and landed classes alike, to the idea that labor was a commodity like any other and would find its price. "The breakthrough of the new political economy of the free market was also the breakdown of the old moral economy of provision" (Thompson 1993: 258).

The pessimistic conclusions about the economy that the classical economists tended to reach had an important impact on thinking about poverty.[10] Malthus saw the poor being affected in large part by forces that were natural rather than social. Similarly, Ricardo saw long-run tendencies in the economy that would not permit the poor to prosper. For them, poverty acquired the inevitability associated with inexorable laws, natural or economic, instead of having the corrigible features typical of phenomena in the social realm. Indeed, an important conclusion in their writings was the idea that policies to help the poor would backfire, an idea that led to reforms in the poor law. Yet the form of this idea – that well-meant policies will be ineffective in the face of inexorable forces – is a lasting legacy of this development. We can see the contrast in its earlier form as the contrast between the mercantilist statesman guiding the ship of state versus the image of the self-regulating economy.[11]

Malthus's *Essay on the Principle of Population* was preceded by Townsend's *Dissertation* ([1786] 1971), which was notable for its linkages between population, subsistence, and policy toward the poor (Polanyi 1957b: 111–129). Townsend based his analysis on competition for food between animals on an island. He concluded, "It is the quantity of food which regulates the numbers of the human species" (Townsend 1971: 38). He then derived from these biological mechanisms a natural order

---

[10] The remainder of this section relies on the discussion of these issues in Dean (1991), and the Townsend and Malthus quotations are from this source.

[11] More recent advocates of policy intervention, such as Keynes, rehabilitated mercantilist ideas while their opponents refer to the power of the invisible hand. This idea is discussed in the next chapter.

in which the more active and industrious members of the species would become masters, and the others servants, if they did not first starve. This biologically derived hierarchy permits agriculture to flourish. The process reaches an endpoint when all productive land is under cultivation and the human species can no longer increase its size. Into this set-up, Townsend inserted the idea of poor relief. He saw it allowing the poor to reproduce without regard to the availability of food for their offspring, which can only be had by diverting the "occasional surplus of national wealth from the industrious to the lazy," thus leading to greater misery and want (Townsend 1971: 40–41). Poor relief not only subverts the "proper channel" of "order and subordination," but encourages indolence, and brings the country to "poverty and weakness" (1971: 42). For Townsend, the poor have "only hunger which can spur and goad them on to labour; yet our laws have said they shall never hunger" – without hunger, there is no "motive to labour and industry" (1971: 23–24).

Poor relief far from being a right of the poor is instead seen as self-defeating and indeed deleterious in its effects. The relation, which we see even today, between opposition to poor relief and a focus on the personal qualities of the poor, is apparent already in Townsend's work. For him, the poor got to be that way because they were lazier and less industrious than those who became rich. Poor relief, which may seem temporarily to help, cannot do so in the long run: "The course of nature may be easily disturbed, but man will never be able to reverse its laws" (Townsend 1971: 42).

Malthus's *Essay* also combines population, food scarcity, and opposition to poor relief. There was a tendency toward over-population as numbers ran up against a more modestly increasing food supply. Since "population must always be kept down to the means of subsistence," a variety of checks to population would have to come into play. These involved either misery (starvation, for example), vice (by which Malthus seems to mean birth control or abortion), and moral restraint in avoiding marriage and procreation (Malthus 1872: 404). From this viewpoint, Malthus claimed, "no distribution of money could possibly raise the general standard of comfort among the poor" (Poynter 1969: 152).[12] A redistribution to the poor might increase the amount of food produced; but the spur that "these fancied riches would give to the population, would more than counterbalance it, and the increased produce would have to be distributed among a more than proportionately increased number of people." The increase of monetary reward would

---

[12] For practical reasons, Malthus and also Ricardo limited their opposition to poor relief to what was politically feasible.

also depress the motive to work (Malthus 1798: 67–68). He therefore concluded that the poor law was self-defeating:

Hard as it may appear in individual instances, dependent poverty ought to be held disgraceful. Such a stimulus seems to be absolutely necessary to promote the happiness of the great mass of mankind; and every general attempt to weaken this stimulus, however benevolent its apparent intention, will always defeat its own purpose. . . (Malthus 1798: 85)

In order to specify more closely how population growth affected the economy, Malthus developed a theory of rent.[13] As population increases, putting pressure on subsistence, land of poorer quality will be brought into cultivation. On the land of least quality, the marginal land, profits and wages will just take up the amount produced. Yet on the land of better quality, the infra-marginal land, landlords will find it possible to realize a rent, which will equal the excess of output per acre over that produced on the marginal land. This will allow wages and profits to be equal on all qualities of land. So the difference in the surplus over labor cost between the marginal and infra-marginal land goes to the landlord, not to workers or farmers. Ricardo used differential rent theory to develop a model of growth (Ricardo 1815/51a and Ricardo 1817/51b). He argued that the rate of return in agriculture determines that of the whole economy, industry included. Profit rates will be equalized among sectors of the economy due to competition. In agriculture, since grain ("corn") is both the input and output, a rate of profit is determined without concern for fluctuations due to variations in prices. Thus "total profits of the farmer regulate the profits of all other trades." With population pressure, however, the agricultural profit rate will decline.

With the progress of society the market price of labour has always a tendency to rise because one of the principal commodities by which its natural price is regulated [viz., corn], has a tendency to become dearer from the greater difficulty of producing it. (Ricardo 1951b: 93)

Here Ricardo had in mind the Malthusian idea that with population pressure, marginal land comes into cultivation, and the rate of profit falls. Competition among farmers for workers might raise the market price of labor, but this would call forth an additional supply of labor, causing the market price to conform to the natural price, determined by the amount of subsistence needed to support a worker. Thus in the classical system, subsistence – even in the presence of growth – ultimately determined the compensation of workers.

[13] Malthus, David Ricardo, Robert Torrens, and Edward West simultaneously discovered theories of differential rent, although Malthus' pamphlet was the first to be published.

Ricardo saw the Poor Law as detrimental even in this vision of the development of the economy. Partly he felt that free markets were preferable, arguing that "wages should be left to the fair and free competition of the market, and should never be controlled by the legislature." If, in this circumstance, the poor were supported by public funds, this would "deteriorate the condition of both poor and rich," the poor because of the inevitable increase in population that higher wages would occasion, and the rich since the maintenance of the poor would absorb "all the net revenue of the country, or at least so much of it as the state shall leave us" (Ricardo 1951b: 106). The opposition to the Poor Law by Malthus and Ricardo helped to create a climate of opinion in which the New Poor Law emerged, though neither played a direct role (Poynter 1969: 328–329). Both authors were vehement in their criticisms of the Poor Law. Ricardo, for example, wrote, "no scheme for the amendment of the Poor Laws merits the least attention which has not their abolition for its ultimate object" (Ricardo 1951b: 107).

The New Poor Law of 1834 was not generous to the poor. It had three key provisions:

1 The able-bodied poor were denied relief unless they entered a workhouse where conditions were less desirable ("less eligible") than those in the worst paying market job. This meant that poor relief was never preferred by workers to market work.
2 There was an end to outdoor relief, i.e., any type of relief such as grants or work given to be done at home. The workhouse was the only avenue for relief.
3 The administration of poor relief was centralized, so that "uniformity and administrative centralization" substituted for "aristocratic self-government." (Halevy 1928: 100)

The New Poor Law, therefore, acknowledged the establishment of a national labor market and, correspondingly, made poor relief a national obligation. Yet in the austerity of its provisions, the new law acknowledged the primacy of market forces to dictate the outcomes for the poor. The principle of less eligibility specifically accommodated market forces and was designed to prevent idleness (Bentham cited in Poynter 1969: 125–126). Notable were the harsh measures to keep people from being idle and the stark reality that relief could never be more attractive than work. With the New Poor Law, the transition from the medieval thought that aid for the poor had its primary basis in a religious impulse to the modern conception that poor relief needed to take into account the workings of the economy was complete. The new law "may be said to represent the decisive victory of the principle that social aid must be subordinated to the needs of the labour market; from that moment, the two were inextricably bound" (Geremek 1994: 239).

The idea of poverty in classical economics both continues and breaks with premodern thinking. While the classical economists no longer see the economy as subordinate to a spiritual purpose, and thus as part of a moral order, the concept of subsistence need carries over into their thinking. Workers are no longer pictured as part of long-term and locally specific employment relations based on craftwork. The differences between workers fade in this setting and workers are homogenized into a class of general laborers. For the most part, the classical economists perceived work as drudgery and those who had to do it as poor even if they received subsistence. The working of labor markets modified the laws in England directed at the poor. The classical economists, specifically Malthus and Ricardo, in their discussions of population and rent, saw the economy settling into a stationary state in a process against which policies to help the poor would be largely ineffective. In this atmosphere, the New Poor Law superseded the Old Poor Law and ushered in harsher policies toward the poor.

# 3    Poverty policy

In this chapter, we explore three examples of how thinking about poverty and unemployment shapes poverty policy. The link forged by the Puritans between personal character and fortune has been particularly influential in shaping poverty policy. Recent and contemporary accounts of poverty often revert to the formula that character is all, circumstances nothing, while other, opposed, accounts formulate the issue in the same framework, simply reversing the causality favored by the Puritans and insisting that circumstance is all and character has nothing to do with the problem. This view, in its more recent formulations, has required that we find ways to measure poverty so that we can gauge the effectiveness of poverty initiatives, the second topic of the chapter. We begin with the problem of unemployment and suggest that the way we understand the causes of unemployment affects who we judge to be responsible and what measures for alleviating poverty are seen as appropriate. We end by considering the idea of individual responsibility and its implications for thinking about poverty policy.

## Self-correcting and crisis prone markets

England's New Poor Law of 1834 responded to the concern that poor relief leads to withdrawal from the labor market and encourages idleness. We see the same concern in the last quarter of the twentieth century in the idea that welfare payments would encourage people to remain outside of the workforce. The modern debate combines elements of the classical conception of a self-regulating economy with the older idea, going back to the Puritans, that misfortune is a personal matter.

In a modern market economy, because much of poverty is associated with unemployment, views of poverty have been associated with views of unemployment. One vision, commonly associated with neoclassical economics, assumes a well-functioning labor market, with any involuntary unemployment being temporary. Some people will be unemployed as shifts occur in the economy, but any unemployment will be followed by a reduction in compensation as the unemployed bid down wages. The lower cost of labor results in an increase in demand for labor and a decrease in supply. Labor demand and supply move closer together, eliminating unemployment. In this view, involuntary unemployment cannot persist in the long run. The only exceptions will be for situations in which there are impediments to well-functioning markets, such as labor unions that elevate wages above the market-clearing levels. Those who hold this view advocate free markets to assure a price for labor consistent with full employment.

If free markets are inconsistent with involuntary unemployment in the long run, then long-run unemployment must be voluntary, which means that the unemployed have chosen their fate. In the language of blame, unemployed workers are responsible for their situation and are therefore undeserving of assistance. The result is a personalization of unemployment, and therefore of poverty, similar to that implied in the older Puritan idea. Thus, belief in the efficacy of free markets is commonly associated with blaming the poor for their situation and with stinginess in poor relief. This view is buttressed by a tendency in the nineteenth and twentieth centuries in advanced countries for the standard of living of workers to improve. As a result, workers have come to be less closely identified with the poor. Consequently, poverty and unemployment are now more firmly linked, even though those who work can still be poor. This contrasts, nevertheless, with the pattern of the heyday of classical economics, where workers were commonly identified poor.

Another historical tendency is the persistence of episodic downturns in economic activity, precipitating rises in unemployment. Some of these could be quite severe, such as the worldwide depression of the late 1920s and early 1930s.[1] Partly because of the persistence of economic declines, a view developed that free markets are crisis prone. Marx, for example, argued that there was an inherent tendency toward imbalance between the sectors of the economy that could result in significant episodes of unemployment, "since . . . balance is itself an accident" (Marx 1981: 571). If so, unemployment might be the rule rather than the exception. Marx's investigations inspired much writing on the crisis prone nature of capitalist development.

---

[1] A third tendency, that economic prosperity is distributed unequally across the world, gave rise to theories of underdevelopment, which we discuss in the next chapter.

Another influential view of economic crisis was that of Keynes. He argued that involuntary unemployment would likely remain in market economies in the absence of government intervention. If money wages fall but prices fall as much or more, real wages would not have fallen, and no increase in employment would result. If unemployment is confined to a single industry and real wages fall only there, the result is likely to be increased hiring in that industry. However, if unemployment is widespread the result is likely to be different. An overall reduction in real wages not only lowers employers' costs, it also reduces the spending power of wage earners. This latter effect depresses demand, thus offsetting the favorable impact of lower wages on expected profit. In general, Keynes argued that a stress on lower wages in thinking about the impact of unemployment on profit expectations ignores the negative effects of reduced income on aggregate demand.

The arguments advanced by Marx and Keynes tended to focus on the workings of the economy as a whole. By contrast, the neoclassical approach focused on the functioning of individual markets and individual decisions. The focus on individual behavior encouraged the tendency to personalize poverty. In the more macroeconomic conceptions, the change of perspective was reflected in a change of the locus of culpability for poverty: the problem rested with the economy as a whole, rather than with individuals. Thus, dealing with the problem became a societal responsibility. Because of this, Keynesian unemployment theory became associated with national intervention in poor relief. If the government had a responsibility for fighting poverty, poverty would need to be defined and measured so that progress in fighting it might be gauged. We now turn to this issue.

## Measurement of poverty

We saw in Chapter 2 that all of the prominent classical economists agreed that the definition of subsistence depends on cultural and social standards. Marx's insistence that subsistence has a moral and historical element is well known. Smith tells us that a worker's necessities include "not only the commodities which are indispensably necessary for the support of life, but whatever the custom of the country renders it indecent for creditable people, even of the lowest order, to be without" (Smith 1937: 821). The process of change in cultural norms was seen to be slow enough that subsistence could be defined. This same way of thinking appears in more contemporary writing about poverty. So, for example, John Kenneth Galbraith (1958) held that while poverty had a physiological basis, "it is wrong to rest everything on absolutes."

People are poverty-stricken when their income, even if adequate for survival, falls markedly behind that of the community. Then they cannot have what the larger community regards as the minimum necessary for decency; and they cannot wholly escape, therefore, the judgment of the larger community that they are indecent.

What is striking in this passage is how the requirements for living are taken to be socially determined. This is what makes subsistence meaningful in the classical setting. While it could change over time, subsistence was given for a well-defined social group. To this extent, the classical conception maintained the idea from medieval times that workers were given subsistence appropriate to their function in society, since workers were seen as helping to reproduce the economic basis of society. But, in the modern period, this conception is more jarring, given the emphasis on individual self-determination rather than on fitting into roles given by social position. It is for this reason that needs, even basic needs, are difficult to define.

This difficulty emerges centrally in the attempts to measure poverty using an approach based on subsistence or basic needs. Rowntree, in his studies of poverty in York, attempted to find the minimum amount "on which physical efficiency could be maintained. It was a standard of bare subsistence rather than living (1941: 102)." This bare-bones approach, which followed the method set by Booth, who coined the expression "line of poverty" in 1886 in his studies of poverty in London, set the pattern that many followed in defining a poverty line. Geremek calls these survival 'norms':

which . . . could be no more than approximations, subject to regional and cultural variation as well as differences in patterns of consumption. It also became evident that it is not only difficult to choose appropriate indices for measuring material poverty; it is equally difficult to separate material poverty from it extra-material aspects, such as educational opportunities, including professional qualifications, and job prospects. (Geremek 1994: 3)

When, in the wake of Harrington's (1962) book arguing that poverty was a large problem in contemporary American society, the US government sought to measure poverty, Orshansky (1965, 1969) devised the method considered in Chapter 1. The central difficulty in this procedure is that it was to be used to show how poverty changed over time, but Rowntree had already shown that poverty line measures were notoriously variable. Rowntree and Lavers (1951) had tried to compare their own poverty estimates for York in 1900, 1936, and 1950. They found an accurate comparison impossible, partly because of a change in what constituted basic needs, but also because changes in the conception of poverty and of in-kind and other provisions by the government.

Rowntree found that 10 percent of York's population was affected by severe poverty in 1900, and this was consistent with the view that poverty was a serious problem at that time, occasioning expenditures by the government to address the matter. Using similar methods, Rowntree and Lavers found the poverty rate to be 1.7 percent in 1950, suggesting that the problem had essentially been solved (Himmelfarb 1991: 384–385). Yet expenditures on poverty in York continued at high rates for several decades. Evidently, the standard for poverty assessment had changed. Given this shifting standard, Rowntree was led to conclude that it was not possible to measure poverty meaningfully over time.

The same issue – substantial variability of the poverty line – arises with respect to Orshansky's measure. Smolensky and Plotnick (1993) calculated what the poverty rate would have been in 1900 using Orshansky's measure (formulated in 1965 and still used in the United States, substantially unchanged). They found that the 1900 poverty rate would have been 80 percent or even higher, depending on assumptions.

If the Orshanksy line were to represent some natural, objective, and constant definition of poverty, the poverty issue in 1900 and earlier would have to have commanded an extraordinary amount of attention. However, while poverty was an important issue at the turn of the century, it was not as important as a near 100 percent poverty rate would suggest. The Orshansky line therefore seems to express a poverty concept that would have had no social or political meaning in 1900. The operative definition of poverty in US society must have risen as average incomes rose between 1900 and 1965. (Bird 1988)

By way of contrast, Hunter's account of 1904 provides an estimate that 13 percent of Americans were living in poverty (Hunter 1904).

In fact, judgments of what constitutes poverty regularly become more liberal as income rises (Kilpatrick 1973). On the basis of surveys asking what is the minimum income needed to get by in a society, Kilpatrick estimates that the resulting poverty lines move up by about three-quarters of the increase in income. Not only do poverty line estimates increase, but they do not increase in equal step with income, suggesting a somewhat increasing tolerance for inequality. Often, researchers and governments abandon an effort to anchor poverty lines in the cost of goods and choose a purely relative approach. Thus, they might classify as poor all those whose earnings are in the bottom quartile of the income distribution (as is done in some European countries). In fact, the United States is one of the few developed countries to use a poverty line based on the cost of goods deemed necessary for living. In Britain, for instance, the method used is to define the poverty line as 60 percent of median income. In 1995, a National Academy of Sciences panel recommended that the United States replace its absolute poverty measure with one that was relative to national incomes and so would change with them (Citro and Michael 1995) but the government did not adopt this report.

These trends have interesting implications for the study of poverty. First, the more relative poverty definitions become, the more likely it is that poverty, thus defined, can never be fully overcome. There is of course the mathematical fact that, unless incomes are equal, not everyone can have an income in the top three-quarters of the income distribution. But, beyond formal considerations is the realization that attempts based on cost methods have to be modified upwards regularly, such that "In literally no country is there a general consensus that transfers have been successful in defeating poverty" (Bird 1998). Poverty becomes a problem that does not have a solution. This goes against the often-stated premise that there is enough affluence to alleviate poverty, a premise that expresses the remarkably persistent conviction expressed in Galbraith's statement that "an affluent society, that is also both compassionate and rational, would, no doubt, secure to all who needed it the minimum income essential for decency and comfort" (1958: 329), in Harrington's statement that poverty alleviation simply depends on providing goods that "our present state of scientific knowledge specifies as necessary for life as it is now lived in the United States" (1962: 179), and in the United Nation's Millennium Development Goal of halving poverty by 2015, which Pogge (2001) claims is a matter of transferring a relatively modest financial sum per year from richer to poorer countries. Thus poverty alleviation is seen as a particularly simple and feasible technical problem (Bird 1998).

Yet the phenomenon of poverty, as measured in these approaches, remains. The poverty line approach recalls the old idea of subsistence, valid for medieval and classical settings, and uses it to draw a line demarcating the poor from the non-poor. But, the application is attempted in the modern era, in which the fixity of needs for which a predetermined payment could be made is lost. The absence of predetermination of need vitiates attempts to set a poverty line. The poverty line either provides nothing close to what is needed to climb out of poverty or it is revised over and over until officials give up trying to value the cost of the required goods, adopting instead a purely relativistic approach, calling all those poor who are in the lowest part of the income distribution. This effectively gives up the war on poverty, since the lowest part of the income distribution will always be with us.

Inadequacies of measurement were not the only reason for the eclipse of the war on poverty. As we discuss further in Chapter 4, identification of poverty with lack of income came into question with the work of Sen. He argued that poverty was a matter of inadequate development of capabilities and not inadequate access to goods or income (Sen 1987). Other authors also cast doubt on the efficacy of income to ward off poverty. A troubling feature of poverty was held to be its intergenerational nature. It was worrying that the poverty of parents seemed to imply the poverty of children, whether defined in terms of income or by outcomes for children. Mayer (1997) tried to clarify whether it was income, or other factors often connected with it, that was to blame. She showed that, holding other factors constant, the correlation between income and outcomes for children was almost zero. Measures of educational achievement such as test scores improved by only a few percentage points when household income doubled (1997: 118–124). The focus on children's welfare was served better by an emphasis on parental involvement and close interaction with children. These new approaches do not ignore material provision; thus health and educational services may be very important to the welfare of children, and income and other material resources do affect capabilities. Yet, by themselves, they are not guarantors of better outcomes for children.

The war on poverty and its associated commitment to transfer and welfare payments was attacked more directly for reasons beyond these. Critics of these programs recalled the Puritan attitude toward achievement and individual responsibility, which is central to attitudes in the United States (Lipset 1990). We see this tendency in the rhetoric that begins with the Margaret Thatcher and Ronald Reagan eras. Part of the impetus behind the attack on welfare payments and the reform of the welfare system was precisely this feeling that the poor deserved their fate.

Those influenced by the kind of thinking to which we have just alluded would reject the idea that the poor represent a social problem, seeing in them evidence not of the failure of social institutions, but of individuals. In the extreme view, this idea leads not in the direction of social policy aimed at alleviating poverty, but away from any such policy, leaving any alleviation of poverty to the private decisions of those individuals and private organizations concerned with the poor. In less extreme versions, this idea leads toward limited policies aimed at correcting the failures in character that prevent individuals from taking advantage of the opportunities afforded them in a free society. This places the onus for poverty on the poor, and especially on their character. In the remainder of this chapter, we explore this idea.

### Will and Character

The idea that poverty is an individual failing casts suspicion on the entire dimension of government concerned with obligation (the so-called "welfare state"), and therefore on the whole idea of poverty policy. Indeed, many contemporary American politicians appeal to this idea when they take a stand against government programs designed to assure a minimum level of living for all citizens. To accept such an obligation would be to reject the idea that how we are situated in this life must be our own doing, and therefore our due. Thus, former Speaker of the House Newt Gingrich tells us:

Precisely because our rights are endowed by our Creator, the individual burden of responsibility borne by each citizen is greater than in any other country . . . By blaming everything on "society," contemporary liberals are really trying to escape the personal responsibility that comes with being an American. If "society" is responsible for everything, then no one is *personally* responsible for anything. (1995: 38–39)

The expansion of government must be limited by the idea of individual responsibility. Government appears as a threat to that idea whenever it seeks to recognize and fulfill social obligations since doing so runs counter to the idea that each individual has ultimate responsibility for him- or herself.

The history of rhetoric and policy aimed at the problem of poverty provides substantial evidence of the attitude considered here. A main theme in policy rhetoric concerning the poverty problem is the concern that government policy will increase and reinforce poverty rather than lead people out of poverty. Those who advocate putting people on welfare to work retrieve the old theme of character and moral failing in their interpretation of poverty.

The idea that any work builds character and discharges social obligations . . . underlies compulsory workfare programs. Their advocates place priority on any work experience regardless of its quality or pay. Forcing women and children into low-wage, dead-end jobs remains preferable to supporting them with public funds. Clearly even new style workfare cannot shed either the equation of work and virtue or the punitive heritage that has rippled through American relief and welfare practices throughout their long and sorry history. (Katz 1989: 231)

For advocates of workfare, failure of character is a, perhaps the, primary element in poverty. To work requires discipline; to remain outside the workforce is to exhibit a failure of discipline. But, not only does work require discipline, it also promotes discipline where discipline is absent or insufficiently developed.

Bill Clinton brings together the themes of workfare and responsibility in his 1998 State of the Union Address:

A strong nation rests on the rock of responsibility. A society rooted in responsibility must first promote the value of work, not welfare. We can be proud that after decades of finger-pointing and failure, together we ended the old welfare system. And we're now replacing welfare checks with paychecks. (Clinton 1998)

In this same address, Clinton refers to "hard-working Americans," and to "parents who work harder than ever." The themes of the Puritans reappear not only in the rhetoric of a conservative Republican Congressman, but also in the rhetoric of a Democratic president.

There is some evidence that these themes resonate with the public, if we consider the strong opposition to welfare spending. In a 1994 survey done by the National Opinion Research Center at the University of Chicago of twenty areas of federal spending, only welfare and foreign aid were widely opposed, with 62 percent of those polled judging welfare spending too high. Yet, while welfare spending ranked second from the bottom in support among spending programs considered, "assistance to the poor" ranked eighth; 59 percent reported that they thought too little was being spent on assistance to the poor, and only 16 percent reported they thought too much was spent on such assistance (Smith 1995). This suggests that strong opposition exists not to the idea of support for the poor, but to the idea of welfare. Then, to replace the idea of welfare with something else, in this case the idea of workfare, replaces a concept laden with negative connotations with one bearing more positive connotations. These connotations are more positive in part because they feed into a set of ideals about work and responsibility so deeply rooted in public consciousness.

In this connection, we should also consider Charles Murray's argument that poverty results from public policy (Murray 1995). His argument and policy recommendations seem to repudiate the idea that poverty constitutes a moral failing (it is a policy failing rather than a moral failing). Yet, for Murray, policy clearly creates dependence by vitiating the necessity that individuals take responsibility for their own welfare. If we follow Murray, we can say that government policy makes it unnecessary for individuals to take responsibility for their well-being. What Murray does not do is suggest that solving the problem of poverty requires character change. While Murray is a political scientist, he adopts the view of most economists that character is an exceedingly simple matter, consisting in the ability to make rational choices.

If incentives created by welfare programs are perverse on practical grounds, they could also be judged perverse on moral grounds since they direct the poor into morally questionable conduct. We might surmise, however, that were social policy eliminated, as Murray suggests, and each individual forced to have recourse to the labor market, the outcome would then be an expression of individual qualities, including those we associate with character. In other words, where social policy offers a superior alternative to the market, it is the external circumstance that determines the outcome for the individual. Then, if we eliminate policy, we return responsibility to the individual. So it follows that returning responsibility to the individual should be the goal of policy, which would best be achieved by the absence of policy. Then, any who fail clearly do so as a result of individual flaws and not external circumstance.

### The rhetoric of the welfare debate

A main theme in the history of welfare policy discussion has been the distinction between the deserving and the undeserving poor, a distinction that rests on a moral judgment. The deserving poor are poor through no fault of their own, but as a result of a loss imposed from outside: loss of employment, or, for women dependent on their husbands, loss of a spouse. The undeserving poor, by contrast, are poor because of their own failure, which can be attributed to their flawed character. Thus, the deserving poor do not deserve to be poor, while the undeserving poor are those who deserve to be poor.

This judgment stems from and continues an early distinction between poverty and pauperism closely related to the ideas about poverty that we find rooted in the Protestant ethic. Thus, the undeserving poor are judged harshly. Indeed, the term "undeserving" refers specifically to those whose condition results from moral failings, who are poor as the result "of willful error, of shameful indolence, of vicious habits" (the Reverend Charles Burroughs writing in 1834, quoted in Katz (1989: 13)).

Michael Katz points out the close connection between the moral definition of poverty and "the identification of market success with divine favor and personal worth" (1989: 14). The early link between the moral definition of poverty and the rise of the free market ideal set the stage for the subsequent formulation of policy, and for the rhetoric of policy debate that continues through the last century. Specifically, Katz links the moral definition of poverty with the literature on the "culture of poverty." The culture of poverty idea "placed in a class by themselves those whose behavior and values converted their poverty into an enclosed and self-perpetuating world of dependence." Those placed in this category remained "different and inferior" (1989: 16).

On the surface, at least, the idea of a culture of poverty did not turn the problem of poverty (or at least of the subset of the poor living in a culture of poverty) into a moral problem, making it the result of a moral failing. Yet, on another level, it carried forward an essential element of the moral rhetoric of poverty. Katz summarizes this element in the following way:

> We can think about the poor as "them" or as "us." For the most part, Americans have talked about "them." Even in the language of social science, as well as in ordinary conversation and political rhetoric, poor people usually remain outsiders, strangers to be pitied or despised, helped or punished, ignored or studied, but rarely full citizens, members of a larger community on the same terms as the rest of us. (1989: 236)

Katz's formulation is an interesting one. Implicitly, it insists that we consider the poor like "us." At the least, it insists we consider the so-called undeserving poor no different from those who are poor due to no "fault" of their own. To get to this point, we must reject the idea that the failings of the poor should be understood in the language of fault, which is the language of virtue and vice, and therefore the language of the moral construction of the world. But, at the same time, we also reject any notion that the poor, especially those who have carried the stigma of the undeserving poor, are, indeed, different from those who can make their way in a market-dominated economic system. There is in this insistence that the poor are us also a denial that the poor are what they are, which is like us, but also different. This denial of the poor has an odd parallel in conservative rhetoric at the time of the Reagan administration, in which a primary theme was that poverty did not exist (Katz 1989: 141).

When denying the existence of the poor failed, conservative rhetoric turned to the idea that poverty resulted from government activism, whose result was to sap the poor of initiative by turning them into dependents of the state (Katz 1989: ch. 4). Katz's denial of the poor leads in a different direction, toward insistence that poverty is not an individual problem at all, but a political problem: "by individualizing poverty, many American social scientists have aided the mystification of its origins, and obscured its politics" (Katz 1989: 237). That is, by considering poverty a matter of character, social scientists and politicians have denied that poverty is a political problem. But, of course, insisting that poverty is a political problem denies that it has anything to do with character.

To insist that the poor are us is to insist either that poverty is not an expression of individual character, or, if it is, that the relevant qualities of character are not limited to the poor. The specific quality of character at stake, as we have seen, is the quality summed up in the term "will." To deny that poverty results from character flaws means either (1) that qualities of character have nothing to do with whether we are poor or not, or (2) that the qualities of character that lead to poverty (or make it more likely) are not flaws. Put in the language of will, it means that either will is unimportant to character or that failure of will has nothing to do with the capacity to cope successfully with the market economy.

Yet, both propositions run up against a difficulty. This difficulty becomes clear enough when we consider the contrasting roles of equal opportunity and community action in the debate over policy to alleviate poverty (Katz 1989: 95–101). Emphasis on opportunity places the burden squarely on the individual, and on that quality of the individual that determines his or her life trajectory. Opportunity only secures the individual against poverty when the individual has the qualities needed to take advantage of opportunity, qualities including those closely associated with will, such as the capacity to take the initiative in discovering and exploiting opportunities.

Emphasis on community action also places emphasis on will, although in a less obvious way. Thus, for some, community participation would overcome "anomie and social disorganization by energizing previously apathetic and disaffected poor people to act on their own behalf" (Katz 1989: 99). It is not far from the hope that policy will stimulate people to act on their own behalf to the idea that policy should have as its result a strengthening of will. Thus, whether oriented toward community action, participation, and politicization, or toward providing opportunities, anti-poverty policy has the invigoration of will as a central element.[2] We will return to the matter of will in poverty policy in Chapter 10.

---

[2] It might be that those who emphasize community action have in mind a collective rather than individual will, though they may not. They may consider community action a vehicle for energizing the individual and developing in him or her a sense of personal agency.

# 4 Income, basic needs, and capabilities

The problem of poverty is a central issue in thinking about underdevelopment. A way to organize this thinking is to ask what the different approaches to development see as missing in the lives of the poor. In broad terms, development thought has seen the poor as lacking income, the ability to satisfy basic needs, or the capabilities to lead a fully human life. In this chapter, we consider each of these possibilities in turn.

## Growth and income

An emphasis on improving outcomes in developing countries by fostering economic growth can follow from neoclassical economics. The neoclassical approach takes as its building blocks information on preferences, endowments, and technology (Debreu 1959). In order for individual welfare to improve, given that preferences are held fixed by assumption, endowments need to increase or technology needs to develop. The emphasis on technological change is consistent with a focus on industrialization. And the idea of increasing endowments is also consistent with growth. Endowments, namely goods and services that individuals have access to for consumption and production purposes, would increase with growth and are themselves inputs for growth. Some of these services can be productive, such as those provided by labor or capital. From this point of view, we can also see why there might be a specific emphasis on increasing the productivity of labor. Hence, there is a neoclassical emphasis on *human capital*, the idea that through education and other means, workers will invest in their own productive capacity. From this viewpoint, investing in human capital, perhaps through education, is the best way to address poverty or poor labor market outcomes (Schultz 1993).

Yet in the several decades following World War II, the immediate emphasis was not on the elaboration of human capital approaches to development. In the wake of independence movements in formerly colonized countries, authors such as Lewis, Mahalanobis, Myrdal,

Nurske, and Rostow recommended industrialization by means of government-led investment in productive capital or the promotion of the importation of capital goods so as to encourage the development of local industry (Rostow 1960). In narrow terms, this emphasis worked. Higher rates of growth and investment did indeed occur. Yet, by the 1970s, there was considerable frustration with this approach. Many of the problems identified with underdevelopment, such as high unemployment, underemployment, and poverty remained. Thus there was frustration with the results of the industrialization approach (Stewart 1985). The situation was summarized in an International Labor Organization document.

> . . . it has become increasingly evident, particularly from the experience of the developing countries, that rapid growth at the national level does not automatically reduce poverty or inequality or provide sufficient productive employment. (ILO 1976: 15)

This frustration with growth and industrialization policy led experts to champion basic needs as the focus of development policy (Green 1976). This approach emphasized the direct physical needs of the poor rather than assuming, as in the industrialization paradigm, that benefits to the poor would simply emerge as by-products of the growth process. Green (1976) and others specified basic needs for food, clean water, clothing, and housing. In addition, they outlined institutional requirements for the provision of basic needs: employment allowing the purchase of items that were not provided publicly; infrastructural investments leading to basic needs fulfillment; and participatory decision-making regarding basic needs provision (Stewart 1985).

## Basic needs

Basic needs imply a hierarchy. To designate some needs as basic implies that they must be supplied first and that other needs follow; those other needs are not strictly necessary. Thus the basic needs idea has two components: an ordering of needs and a dividing line between those that are basic and those that are not. Both of these components have been problematic. The very term "basic" suggests a problem. If something is a need, it is necessary. Necessary things do not admit of further distinctions so far as necessity is concerned, but the word "basic" implies some needs are not really needs at all. It seems awkward to have needs – necessary things after all – that are not basic. Hence the category of wants or luxuries or conveniences is appealed to, and no one speaks of non-basic needs.

It has been difficult for authors championing the idea of basic needs to come up with a list of such needs. Griffin (1986) attempted to distinguish between needs and wants. He argued that needs are wants "that are both necessary and sufficient for a recognizably human existence" (1986: 53). He thus links needs to what is irreducibly human, in a way similar to that of others who have approached this problem. Indeed, his list of needs resembles those of others, e.g., Braybrooke (1987). Yet he argues that needs are more objective than wants, and it may be possible within a given society, rather than cross-culturally, for people to agree about what is needed and therefore sufficient for a human existence (Lane 1991: 439). However, Griffin's attempt is inconsistent. Needs cannot both be an irreducible feature of all humans and also be societally specific. To combine the two criteria makes the quality of humanness societally specific rather than general. Griffin's attempt shows the difficulty of the project of identifying basic needs. Indeed others who have tried to define the concept of basic needs more precisely have found it difficult to do. A writer sympathetic to the human needs approach admits that "the abstract word, needs, is never clearcut" (Clark 1990, cited in Douglas et al. 1998: 206). The matter of identifying basic needs is similar to determining a poverty line – a level of income that divides the poor from the non-poor. You are poor if your income does not permit you to buy the basics of life. As we saw in the last chapter, this determination has never had a convincing basis.

Douglas and her coauthors argue that what is striking about the distinction arising from basic needs is that it seems to be based on an "antique psychology" that saw persons as having a spiritual element in an animal body (Douglas et al. 1998: 200). The animal side must be satisfied before spiritual, artistic, and other "higher" needs are attended to. The spiritual element is thus an add-on to the more basic, constitutive animal element. From this point of view, basic needs are devoid of cultural, intellectual, spiritual, or artistic concerns. Life is first of all a biological fact, and so the necessities of life are at bottom biologically based. This impulse to invoke a universal biological core as the determinant of needs is expressed frequently in the abstract, but difficult to make concrete. For example, in talking about subsistence (an idea related to basic needs), the classical economists allowed a "moral and historical" element in the determination of subsistence. If subsistence in physical terms changed overtime, it could not be simply biological, since biological needs would be stable.

We have seen that the concept of basic needs suggests the idea of a needs hierarchy. Basic needs must be satisfied first. Once they are satisfied, other needs may assert themselves. This idea was elaborated by Maslow (1943), who argued that a need at a higher level becomes urgent only after lower needs are satisfied. Different variations of his model exist. But a five-level hierarchy is representative: physiological needs are satisfied first, followed in order by safety, belongingness and love, esteem and, finally, self-actualization. The hierarchy is often represented as a pyramid, with physiological needs at the base and self-actualization at the apex.

While Maslow's idea has been influential, it has also been criticized both conceptually and as not conforming to evidence. Lea *et al.* (1987: 145–146) review the tests in the psychological literature of Maslow's hypotheses. They find little evidence of an elaborate structure of needs; and, contrary to Maslow's supposition, needs that he supposes occur in an order, actually occur concurrently. Related concerns about Maslow's hierarchy of needs refer to non-Western cultures where the pyramid does not seem to hold. Douglas *et al.* (1998: 229) refer to Sahlins (1988) and other anthropologists who point out that hunter-gatherers had very different priorities from those suggested by Maslow. In those societies, much time was devoted to "cave painting, cosmetics, recitation, dancing, ritual, and other self-expressive activities," just the sort of things that are near the apex of Maslow's pyramid and to which relatively little attention should be paid by people in poor societies. Such examples, which can be multiplied and made more current, suggest that a focus on basic needs, found at the base of Maslow's pyramid, misses people's real priorities.

Such problems with defining basic needs imply that a larger issue is involved. Recall the discussion of subsistence and the transition from the premodern to the modern outlook (in Chapters 1 and 2). In the medieval system, roles were well defined. Each occupation or vocation required a certain set of instruments, tools, or other accoutrements to allow the job to be done. In return, there was a culturally defined subsistence provided for work of each type. In the medieval setting, then, needs *could* be defined at the outset. With the development of undifferentiated work and the advent of a general labor market in the seventeenth and eighteenth centuries, the instruments of work became subject to technological change motivated by the capitalist drive for profit, and so acquired a logic of their own. However, the concept of subsistence – now to be applied to a general laborer – remained. Again, while work was transformed, subsistence could be defined and played a definite role in the compensation of workers. With the arrival of modern conceptions, however, several things changed, vitiating attempts to define subsistence. With modernity there are continual upheavals in ways of life and patterns of consumption. There is no presumption that one is born into or destined for a particular way of life. Rather, individuals discover ways of life. In this setting, it is naturally difficult to define either subsistence or a universally acceptable set of basic needs.

Moroever, in the modern setting, a list of goods misses the point. In the medieval period, a set of tools and subsistence implies a particular way of life. The Old Poor Law (discussed in Chapter 2), in its provisions for outdoor relief, tried to recreate the medieval provision of means of work to those who were out of work. In the era of classical economics, subsistence also implied a type of work and a way of life, albeit one that was appropriate for generalized labor. Where underlying work was not available, as with the Old Poor Law, compensation was provided equivalent to what working would generate. With the New Poor Law, providing a minimum amount meant to cover basic needs does not come close to recreating what has been lost when someone no longer has work. Providing a set of goods, or an amount of money with which this list can be acquired, makes possible a mere shadow of the life that has been lost. What needs to be recreated is not the material goods associated with a general conception of life (basic needs) but the form of life itself (which of course will have material requirements). This means that the basic needs idea misses the point or the goal of a modern conception of life. In its concern with goods, it can provide at best a shriveled version of what people require.

What is striking about basic needs theory is that it presumes that needs are known. This is inconsistent with the flux that we expect in a process of development and the resulting changes in personal development that would ensue. In the basic needs conception, needs are divided into a portion that is unchanging and universal (basic needs) and another that is variable (wants). The fixity refers, of course, to basic needs. While there is a tendency to regard basic needs as biological, and therefore given by matters of physiology, lists of basic needs always go beyond what is strictly biological. It is difficult to conceive of humans as having only biological requirements. Even those needs that might be thought of as being the most biologically based, such as food, have cultural, social, and temporal elements of variability in them. Similar to the subsistence notion of the classical economists, there is a "moral" or "historical" element of variability to apparently basic needs. Thus, the conception of basic needs requires the kind of fixity of needs that seems to be at such odds with the flux of modern life, or even of life in a process of development toward more modern forms.

## Capabilities and Human Development

We have argued that a focus on basic needs shortchanges the poor. It also misses the point of human development in a modern setting. Another way of expressing this objection is to say that the basic needs approach is excessively based on commodities as alleviators of poverty. It is primarily on this basis that advocates of the capabilities approach have criticized the basic needs idea. After all, someone whose basic needs were satisfied would still be poor if the person did not display the *beings and doings* of a fully developed human being. The basic needs idea concentrates on what people have rather than on what they might become or do.

Amartya Sen and his collaborators have contrasted a commodity-based definition of the standard of living with a view emphasizing human functioning (Sen 1987). In a normal process of development, capabilities that all humans have the potential to develop and exercise are realized in play, work, education, conversation, family life, friendship, and so on. While all people have the potential to develop these capacities, defects in the family, social, or economic environment may be such that these potentialities do not become actual. Thus malnutrition or lack of good preventive health care may prevent a child from taking part in play or benefiting from an education. Lack of opportunities for employment may harm the development of many. Psychological problems, whether they are caused by traumatic events such as war and general violence, or by occurrences in a person's upbringing or intimate life, may similarly present obstacles to development. Thus, a series of institutional, social, and family requirements need to be in place for successful development (Little 2003: 17–18).

The focus in the human development approach is on what people can do or become, not on what they have. Yet this viewpoint encompasses what seems to be of value in the neoclassical and basic needs approaches. The emphasis on choice in the neoclassical approach finds a foothold here. When the background requirements for good development are present, people are able to devise and pursue a worthy plan for their lives. Here, their ability to choose freely means determining the type of life they want to have. Thus choice and freedom are important, but not in ways that easily fit into the neoclassical framework. Likewise, the human development approach addresses the desire expressed in the basic needs idea that important needs are satisfied in a process of development. When people have chosen a way of life and are pursuing it successfully, their needs are satisfied. It seems beside the point to inquire whether people here have sufficient quantities of specified goods. So, with its concern with human flourishing, the capabilities idea addresses the valuable insights that are contained in these other approaches (Little 2003: 19).

Thinking about poverty in terms of human development rather than commodities transforms the meaning of poverty. If people were fully able to realize their capacities as human beings, the matter of riches and poverty measured in terms of commodities or incomes would become secondary. In this view, income and commodities are important not for their own sakes but *because* their absence might retard development. This insight gives us the proper ordering: the end is human development and commodities; income and choice are means to it. Thus needs fulfillment is important to the extent that it allows for human flourishing. Free choice is important in the same way. But an attempt built on basic needs or preference alone will only provide a limited approach to the problem of human development.

The capabilities approach, therefore, comes closer to offering an adequate theory of persons and their development. Indeed, we build on the capabilities approach and elaborate its relation to poverty in Chapters 6 and 7. In order to set the stage for this elaboration, we now consider some aspects of the work of Martha Nussbaum, another contributor to this approach, and of Amartya Sen, more closely.

Nussbaum attempts to delineate universal human capabilities – capabilities without which people cannot rightly be called human. She holds that we can say what is important for a human life independently of historical and cultural variations.[1] Another way of saying this is that people have and have had the same capacities for functioning (so far as this functioning is related to being human) in all social and cultural settings. Nussbaum specifies not only a general account of well-being but also its components. The dimensions of value concern autonomy, health, relationships, and other matters; they include a life of normal length, good health, integrity of the body, the use of thought, imagination and the senses, the ability to display emotions and to engage in practical reasoning, the ability to socialize and affiliate with others, to show a concern for other species, to play and to have control over one's environment (Nussbaum 2001: 78–80). Her contention is that these dimensions of human ability "exert a moral claim that they should be developed" (2001: 83). The goal is not to ensure actual functioning but to ensure the capability for that functioning. While Nussbaum does indicate the areas making up a good life, she certainly allows that there are many ways in which each of these areas of functioning could be

---

[1] The way that these capabilities might manifest themselves in precise detail will vary, but not so their importance or general character.

realized in individual instances. Thus, while play is important, the particular sort of play is not.

An important question that needs to be posed for Nussbaum's argument is the following: Can this idea about development's end be reconciled with the central ideal of a modern society, which is the ideal of freedom emphasized in Sen's recent formulations of the capabilities approach? This question will be of special importance for our discussion of poverty, where emphasis is placed on opportunities yet undetermined, and ways of life that are not prescribed for the individual. In subsequent chapters, we explore this matter more fully, and suggest how the capabilities idea can be both extended, and in some ways reconceived, to be made more fully consistent with the ideal of freedom.

## Universality

The issue of whether approaches to poverty may be considered universal has been implicit in much of our discussion up to this point, but takes on special importance in development contexts, where concepts such as basic need and capability play a large role. To address it more closely, we might begin with the distinction between subsistence and basic needs. The classical economists identified subsistence as what was needed to support life at a particular place and time. The content of subsistence would vary with changes in culture and social norms. The list of subsistence goods was not universal, but determined by custom. This is why subsistence identifies the recipient's place in the structure of society. Referring as it does to custom, the concept of subsistence is concerned not only with physical survival but also with cultural appropriateness. In this, subsistence as used by the classical economists shows its affinity to the same term as applied in the medieval setting, where "Each member . . . must receive the means suited to its station, and must claim no more" (Tawney 1962: 23).

With basic needs, we find a different ambition expressed, which is to identify those goods that all people in all settings must have. As we saw earlier in this chapter, it is difficult to divide those goods that are basic from those that are not, even if the categories of basic need, such as food, shelter, health, and education, seem compelling in the abstract. For, in order to make a list appropriate for development policy, the general areas of basic need have to be made specific and this is difficult to do. In order to compile a list that is as universal as possible, the promulgators of the basic need idea sometimes prune away needs that do not seem absolutely fundamental, thus ending up with what is ostensibly needed for physical survival. Even this is difficult to do. And, even if it were possible, the result would likely shortchange the poor by misestimating what they need to move out of poverty.

These difficulties suggested to supporters of the capabilities approach to human development that the emphasis on a list of particular goods was misguided. Their focus, as we saw above, is on what humans could be and do. The focus is on identifying "What are the forms of activity, of doing and being, that constitute the human form of life?" (Nussbaum 1995: 72). Once we identify these activities, we can determine the capabilities that allow humans to undertake them. Nussbaum considers these capabilities to be universal. Whatever the particular ways of life we might observe in different cultures, people living in them can distinguish ways of life that are human from those that are not. She argues that when we look across societies there is substantial coincidence among different views of what makes a life human. In other words, the conception of what makes a life human exhibits an underlying universality.

Among the capabilities that Nussbaum identifies as being universally held are those of autonomy and the ability to conceive and carry out a plan for one's life. We might doubt that this is a truly universal capability, given that it involves overthrowing the bonds of tradition, which tend toward prescribing a customarily determined way of life. We might especially doubt that this is true for the capability for freedom, which undergirds our own approach to poverty, since we link its importance to the advent of modernity. Be that as it may, the issue of universality that Nussbaum raises brings to the fore important questions.

To deal with these questions, it will be helpful to distinguish between two meanings of "universal" (Levine 2001: 31–35). The first is seen in the basic needs and capabilities approaches when they take to be universal what is common to diverse societies and cultures. Universal needs or capabilities apply in all settings and therefore are present before the factors that shape the particular setting. Following the second meaning, we might interpret universal differently, to mean unrestricted in application to a particular setting. This interpretation emphasizes the idea of the universal as what is potential rather than what is actual and has already taken on a particular form. The second meaning of universal focuses our attention on the freedom of possibilities yet to be determined.

Since our emphasis here is on the universality of the norm of freedom, it is natural for us to think of universality as a potential rather than as a common quality in the diverse shapes of what already exists. After all, to conceive and carry out a plan of life means to discover something that does not already exist. This is possible only in societies that allow for it, and since many do not, the ideal of freedom cannot be considered universal in Nussbaum's sense, though it might be considered universal in the second sense suggested above. But, does the absence of universality in Nussbaum's sense mean that the norm of freedom has no special status, given that it is historically and culturally specific?

To approach this matter, let us consider the issue of cultural diversity. Over the past several hundred years, cultures have increasingly come into contact with one another. Cultural isolation has given way to societies that are culturally diverse. Among the reasons for this trend are the transformation of traditional ways of life by capitalism, the internationalization of trade and production, the development and diffusion of modern media and means of communication, and dislocations caused by migration and war. When groups or societies come into contact with one another, comparisons of ways of life cannot be avoided. In contrast to the situation in an isolated traditional society, the members of a traditional society placed in a diverse setting can see the possibility of a different sort of life. Even if they cannot leave the traditional society, they can imagine what it might be like to do so.

Ways of life in a particular society have a hold over members because of their claim to be universal. Where different options are seen to be possible, this claim comes into question.

The commitment of culture to control ways of life – modes of interaction and attachment; the meaning of human experience; appropriate beliefs about self, other, and the surrounding world; and so on – must be undermined when imagining other ways of life becomes a possibility. (Levine 2001: 33)

This breakdown of the claim to universality that was possible for isolated cultures leads to three possibilities. In one, associated with the term "multiculturalism," the claim to universality is abandoned, and moral judgment is grounded in the standards of particular communities, whose purview is limited just to themselves. Yet, while each culture has authority over its members, each culture is meant to respect the prerogatives of other cultures. Thus cultures are forced to acknowledge the legitimacy of the authority of other cultures over their own members. This possibility thus seeks to combine local authority with relativism. But to accept the difference implied by relativism fully is to undermine even local authority. This might be seen in the tension that would be faced by fundamentalist religious groups trying to agree to each other's authority. It is difficult for cultures to exist in this framework and retain what they find to be distinctive about themselves. In addition, multicultural societies are only ideally loose amalgams of autonomous cultures. The fact that different cultures exist within a society means that aspects of the legal and political framework must be shared. To the extent that this framework derives more clearly from one of the cultures in the society means that all cultures must accept its legitimacy for their own members. Thus even the idea that cultures determine ways of life completely for their own members is only ideally true.

A second possibility is for societies to attempt to recover the state of isolation that existed before cultures came to live side by side. They may strive to isolate themselves from the rest of the world so as to make the possibility of comparison remote. Or they may try to destroy or demonize (rather than respect) the cultures that seem to present their members with alternative ways of life. Fundamentalist societies are more likely to choose this option than an option in which they acknowledge the local authority of other cultures and face the inevitable comparisons between cultures. In this situation, there is only one possibility for universality. That is, the only possibility for universality is to implement Nussbaum's procedure. This is to search across cultures for aspects of ways of life that are held in common. Yet, this commonality is unlikely to arrive at what the cultures feel is significant about human life. Given that some cultures feel a fundamental hostility toward others and stress that their ways of life are distinctive and separate, a procedure that tries to find what is common runs up against the tendency to isolate and separate. There may indeed be commonalities, but the commonalities are not likely to include what cultures feel is important to being human.

There is also a third possibility. In the first two alternatives, the particularity of separate cultures is maintained. Either cultures exist within a society that tries to combine local hegemony and respect for cultures; or cultures are isolated or hostile to one another but we nevertheless try to find what they have in common and equate that with what is universally human. The third possibility denies cultures the power to determine the practices and beliefs of individuals. Rather than deriving his or her way of life directly from the forms dictated by culture, individuals discover or create those ways of life. An individual may choose from what is available already, or discover a new pattern; but it is the individual who determines what sort of life to lead. Culture no longer prescribes ways of life; but culture permits and fosters an environment in which ways of life may be discovered. When culture no longer determines ways of life, we can speak of culture as being universal in our second sense of the term, since it represents not already known and determined ways of living, but the potential to develop, discover, and create. Such a culture is appropriate to a society organized around the ideal of individual autonomy and self-determination.

Aspects of the other two possibilities may be found in the third alternative. Because ways of life are chosen, diverse ways of life will likely develop. Thus the often-stated aim of multicultural society – diversity – results but without the hegemony of culture over the individual. Individuals can only exploit the opportunity freedom affords in an appropriate institutional setting and where they have the capacity to turn the potential into the realities of their concrete, particular lives. They must have both the external institutions of freedom and the internal capacity for freedom. The norm of freedom does, then, retain a special status with regard to universality. We may consider humans to be born with the potential to develop this capacity. Thus, if the capacity for freedom is not universal in Nussbaum's sense, the potential might be. However, the potential may not be developed, so the capability will not be universal; nor will the significance of the norm of freedom be universally accepted (Levine 2001: 152, n. 13). In the next chapters, we discuss the norm of freedom, the development of the capacity for freedom, and its relation to creativity and skilled work.

*Part II*

# 5   Needs, work, and identity

## From moral order to individual right

Subsistence need carries the moral authority of the community. Because it carries this authority, subsistence need has power over the member, the power to determine what the member needs and how that need will be satisfied. The community's power over its members carries with it an obligation to assure, so far as possible, that the member's needs, which are also the community's needs, are satisfied. The member has his or her obligation to do work of a particular kind and, more generally, to perform his or her designated function. And the community has its obligation to assure, so far as possible, the livelihood of its members. In a world where the community no longer carries the moral authority to determine need and how need is satisfied, what replaces the community's moral authority and the system of mutual obligation that goes with it is the ideal of individual right. The growing hegemony of this ideal has the most far-reaching implications for the theory of need and the idea of poverty. To see where the ideal of right takes the theory of need, we will first consider that ideal more closely.

The language of right links conduct to volition. In a moral order, conduct is determined by external imperatives. In a system of individual rights, conduct originates in individual will. To have a right is to be able to act at our will, rather than being subject to the will of others or determined by natural imperatives. As individuals, we are driven by a variety of forces both internal and external. These are the forces of need and want, and the subtly and not so subtly coercive forces of our social institutions and social relations. To will is to be able to say no to those forces, to not act in the face of the various imperatives operating on us.

Not acting can be considered the prelude to action, so will in this sense is not synonymous with doing nothing, though doing nothing can also be an act of will. When we act though we might not, our action has a special meaning in that it now originates within. We are its source and origin, even if, in the end, we decide to act so as to satisfy a need or conform with a social norm, for example.

We can understand something important about will if we consider for a moment what we do when we do not act. After all, if nothing happens when we do not act, will can, at best, only negate action. We could never will anything. What makes action the expression of will is this something that takes place during the moment when we suspend the forces impelling us to act. This something that occurs during the moment when those forces are suspended is the turning inward we will refer to as "dwelling in the mind." We will speak of will, then, as a moment in the course of our affairs when we turn inward, and dwell in the mind rather than in the world outside. The ability to turn inward and then act from that basis is what the psychoanalyst Donald Winnicott refers to as the "doing that arises out of being" (Winnicott 1986: 39).

Dwelling in the mind refers to the state of finding comfort in our experience of our selves. Our ability to find comfort in the experience of the self depends on our ability to make a positive emotional investment in the self. When we do so we have, to use Winnicott's language, "a basic place to operate from" (1986: 39). Having a place to operate from means that what we do expresses something intrinsic about us, and is not essentially the response to external stimuli. This will no doubt seem an odd way to look at things, especially in light of the normally active connotations of will and right. It is, nonetheless, important to understand that, at their core, both ideas depend on our capacity to begin from the inside, from within the mind, rather than from imperatives originating elsewhere.

Many would deny, and have denied, that the negation of need's power to determine conduct required for the act of will and meaningful exercise of right is possible, some because of their convictions about the natural imperatives that drive us as members of a species, others because of their convictions about our social determination as members of a group or community. The idea of basic need tends to encourage this denial of the possibility of suspending need's power. We will not engage this issue directly here, except to note that if we are, in fact, wholly driven in this way by social or natural imperatives, then the idea of right is little more than an illusion.

To understand will and right, then, we must first understand what goes on in the mind during the moment when those external forces acting on us are suspended. Part of the answer to the question of what goes on in the mind at this moment would be the activities of thinking and imagining. If willing means exercising the capacity to think, and especially to imagine, then it means living in a way that is not wholly dominated by what Freud refers to as the "reality principle," which expresses the external imperatives of living in a world, both natural and social, which we neither create nor control. In the mind, it is possible to live the imagined life, which is a life constrained only by the limits of our imagination. The reality principle refers to life in a world that exists independently of our imagination.

If we understand this relationship between will and imagination, we can begin to understand the relationship between will and human creativity, which is essential if we are to appreciate the significance of the ideal of right. For this, we offer an example from Robert Inman's novel *Old Dogs and Children*, in which a man and his young daughter have the following exchange:

"Will this road have macadam on it?" She tried to imagine a ribbon of black stuff all the way to Columbus.

> "Of course."
> "How do you know?"
> "Because I can see the future," [her father] said simply.
> She looked up at him curiously. "How do you do that?"

"Nothing hard about it. You just think about the way you would like things to be, and then you start working to make them that way, and that's the future. One day every street in this town" – he waved in the general direction of town – " will be paved with macadam. I'll see to it." (Inman 1998)

In this vignette, will links two realities, one imagined and subjective, the other real in an objective world. Imagination produces an idea of what might be. This idea is the raw material for willing. Without the imagined reality, dwelling in the mind produces nothing, and will has no meaning.

Originally, and most importantly, the ideal of right is meant to provide a framework for a world that has space for individuals to have and to realize their own individual fantasies or imaginative constructions of reality so far as these do not impinge on others. That is, the world of rights is not one imagined world, but many. Right protects this system of many imagined worlds. This is what makes the ideal of right attractive. It also connects the ideal of right to living in a world where there are many cultures and many communities, but none that can easily claim the moral authority to prescribe ways of life for its members.

Of course, right does more than protect the imagined world; it also secures the possibility that we might realize what begins in our imagination. This is the possibility that we might live what we had imagined, make real what we imagined might be. In this sense, right relates to the active moment of will, the moment when we will something rather than simply suspending the power of need to determine what we do. Our rights assure that we are free to shape our lives according to our will.

### From known to unknown need

When right replaces the moral authority of community, needs are not already known. Put another way, the subsistence needs of the member of the community no longer carry authority over the individual. We do not know what individuals need in the way the community knows what its members need. But, not only is need unknown to the community, it is also unknown to the individual who, having lost his attachment to the subsistence and to the position in the social order implied by it, must now discover what he needs. This moment of not knowing is necessary if need is to express individual self-determination rather than the demands of group membership.

The idea that our right is to not satisfy a need is closely linked to the idea that people do not know what they need. Not knowing what we need is a peculiar state to be in, and one not at all typical of human experience. It is the state typical of life in what we might refer to as the modern world. What distinguishes life in the modern world is not what we now know that previously we did not, though that is substantial. What is important is not what we know, but what we do not know. The modern world is characterized by not knowing, just as the earlier shape of life was characterized by what was already known. Not knowing creates the space for creativity and gives meaning to the institutions of freedom.

This means that a system must be put in place for producing and distributing the things people need when need is not already known. Such a system would express self-determination rather than embeddedness in the community and would facilitate individual self-discovery. So far as, within this system, individuals take the initiative in discovering what they need and in seeking the means to satisfy their need, the determination of need and the pursuit of the means to satisfy need can be considered acts of will. When we consider need satisfaction an expression of will, we should expect institutions of right to play a primary role, so that need satisfaction will involve the exercise of right.

The right most naturally and easily linked to the idea of self-discovery and needs yet to be determined is the right to own and use property. By owning and using property, we create a world of our own, a world within which to exercise and express our capacity for imaginative construction. Respect for property right also means that others enter our world, as we enter theirs, only by invitation. This is not the only significance property right has. It can also underwrite the pursuit of wealth for its own sake, and more generally, ownership of wealth without regard to need. This other use of property is vitally important in modern economies, but it is not our primary concern here. Whatever the other uses of property, it remains essential in a world of imagined realities, a world where we are, to a significant degree, free to shape our lives according to our will.

When we make need satisfaction a matter of individual or private willing, we make the objects used to satisfy need individual or private property. Because of this, respect for private property is implicated in the ideal of self-discovery, which includes the idea of needs not already known. Respect for private property means that its use is subject to the will of its owner, and this means that acquisition or alienation of property is through voluntary transactions, especially exchange. Systems of exchange, or market systems, realize the ideal of self-determination of need, and, indeed, are designed at least in part to do so. The importance of market systems in assuring that need expresses self-determination does not prejudge the question of the limits of the market and the role of government (see Levine 1995, 2001). It simply reflects the fact that a vital purpose of the market is enabling individuals to discover needs not already known and determined for them, and that a well-designed market system does this work well.

A long-standing argument in political economy links markets to individual self-determination by linking markets to the use of decentralized information. One of the main reasons information is decentralized is that it pertains to the individual and not the community as a whole. The most famous version of the argument linking markets to decentralized information comes to us from Adam Smith who ties the virtue of markets to their dependence on the judgment of the individual owner of capital. Thus, according to Smith, "every individual, it is evident, can, in his local situation, judge much better than any statesman or lawgiver" what species of industry "is likely to be of the greatest value" (1937: 423).[1] Because knowledge is decentralized, institutional arrangements for making effective use of that knowledge must place decision-making into the hands of the individual units.

The argument applied by Smith to production also applies to the matter of what is to be produced. Smith does not apply it in this way

---

[1] This argument was elaborated by Friedrich Hayek in his essay on markets as mechanisms for using knowledge (Hayek 1945). Contrary to the assumption sometimes made, this argument for the use of markets does not, in itself, resolve the matter of the role of government, and especially of the desirability of government regulation of industry.

presumably because of his attachment to a subsistence theory of need. Given the subsistence theory of need, while knowledge about investment opportunities may be decentralized, knowledge about what people need would not be. Decentralized knowledge of need is, however, implied when subsistence needs give way to individual needs, which are not prescribed or predetermined, but yet to be discovered. This is an important result, but it gets in the way of an attempt to define poverty as the failure to satisfy known needs and poverty policy as provision of known needs to those who are unable on their own to acquire the necessary means.

The difficulty to which we have just alluded raises an important question: does severing the tie between need, community, and subsistence make needs arbitrary, nothing more than the preferences sometimes favored by economists when they describe the work of markets? Put another way, does the fact that needs are individual needs, determined by a process of individual self-discovery, make them nothing more than preferences? Or, can we still speak of need, and therefore hold out the hope that we might also speak of poverty in relation to need even where needs are not prescribed because they are yet to be determined?

One possibility is to continue to consider poverty the inability to satisfy need, but to treat need as an individual matter. What makes the failure to satisfy individual needs a real loss, so that the term impoverishment might apply, is the connection of those needs to individual identity. This link is analogous to the link between cultural subsistence and poverty. The inability to acquire the cultural subsistence has significance because it also means loss of identity, the difference being that in the latter case the loss is of group identity, while in the former it is of individual identity. The main point is that the quality of experience that lends a force of necessity to need not implied in preference is the link to identity, whether we conceive identity as an individual matter or not. If we are to attempt to link the failure of need satisfaction to poverty by introducing the idea of individual identity, we will need to clarify how we are using that term and how it might apply to the problem at hand.

### Identity

For the individual, having an identity means having at least the following qualities (Erikson 1980):

1 Self-awareness
2 Continuity of being across time

3 The investment of meaning in a connected life experience
4 Finiteness or boundedness
5 Recognition.

To have an identity is to be aware of one's self. Organisms can exhibit continuity through time without having identity in this sense. Thus, we can identify plants, animals, even inanimate objects, but this does not mean that they have an identity in the sense considered here. Having an identity does not begin with being known by others, but with being known by oneself. Being known by oneself is the prelude and precondition for being known by others as someone who has an identity, is well defined, and therefore identifiable. Because of this, identity is linked to the special internal quality of self-awareness.

Individuals may have the capacity to stand outside of themselves, to self-evaluate, to gain and use self-knowledge. But, they may not. Self-awareness is closely associated with the capacity to judge possibilities according to their fit with capabilities and ideals. In the absence of self-awareness, we will find vulnerability to external influence. Self-awareness is thus closely linked to dwelling in the mind, since it is our capacity to do so that enables us to make conduct expressive of will and thus to limit the influence of external forces. Failure of self-awareness can foster impulse-driven behavior, no matter how apparently planned conduct might appear to be. To realize an identity through action in the world means we are not driven by impulse, but, rather, that our conduct has a self-reflective quality. This does not imply that all conduct must arise out of conscious reflection on the self, or that impulse can have no part in life, but only that impulse acting must be consistent with the self as a creative principle and the origin of creative living.

As a direct expression of the quality of self-awareness, having an identity means that experiences and actions are connected because they have a meaning, most importantly to the self. There is, then, an emotional investment in the sequence of experiences and actions, which is valued as a whole (Loewald 1980: 351). This capacity to make an emotional investment in the person as a whole is vital for identity. Indeed, as implied in much of the language used here to speak about identity, having an identity is an expression of a particular quality of the person also referred to as having or being one's self. The difference is that identity refers to the complex sequence of experiences, actions, and relationships, taken concretely, that make up a life, while self refers to that inner quality of being that establishes the meaning and connectedness of those experiences, actions, and relationships. Put another way, the term self refers to the potential or capacity for investment in a life experience, while identity refers to the salient concrete elements of that experience.

We can also say, then, that identity is a meeting point of the imagined and the possible. To have an identity is to have imagined what might be. Without this moment of imagining, our connection to experience would be wholly adaptive. If the moment of identity is the moment that makes experience our own, then it is also the possibility and expression of creative living.

While identity is linked in this way to creativity, it is also linked to boundaries. To have an identity is to be something concrete, the realization of a potential in a particular life experience. Being something, of course, means not being everything else. Having an identity means knowing what we are and what we are not. Awareness of limits, or finitude, is an essential element of identity.

That identity represents a meeting point of the imagined and the possible means that identity connects the inner world to the world outside. Those qualities of identity that enable us to see ourselves in what we do also allow others to see us, thus making the self real in a world of others. Its close connection to the process of identification expresses this aspect of identity. To shape an identity through identification with others means that our identity must in some ways be shared, no matter how personal it may also be. Identity connects self to other by connecting the inner world to the world outside.

## Impoverishment and identity

In shaping our identity, we may play a more or less active role. The less actively we shape our identity, the more we take it in from outside, the more that identity is ascribed to us rather than an expression of our unique presence of being. Group identity tends to be ascribed in this sense. Ascription of identity is closely linked to prescribed ways of life and prescribed need. It is the process by which need is prescribed for the group member. The ascribed identity displaces any initiative for shaping a life originating within the individual, which is to say, originated by the activity of the individual self. Such an identity is not the concrete expression in a particular lived life of a self, but the concrete expression in a lived life of the group. The process of ascription then grounds the concept of subsistence, and the concepts of poverty related to it.

An ascribed identity carries a burden for the group member so far as he or she aspires to an individual life outside the group, since it challenges the legitimacy of the impulse to shape a life, and therefore an identity, according to an internal process. For the ascribed identity to prevail against the impulse toward creative living, the latter must be judged in some way unacceptable. Denigrating the impulse to develop a personal identity makes possible the dominance of an ascribed identity. There is in this denigration of the impulse for creative living a kind of impoverishment.

Not only, however, can the impulse toward a personal identity and creative life be denigrated in service of the ascribed identity of the group, the ascribed group identity can also be the object of attack. When this happens, and the ascribed identity is denigrated as in some way unworthy, the individual suffers a two-fold blow to his or her self-esteem. First, the denigration of the aspiration to a personal identity is felt as an attack on the value of the self, and when that personal identity is replaced by an ascribed identity that has been devalued, the attack on the worth of the self is multiplied. Thus, membership in an ethnic group disparaged by the larger culture and society in which we live, imposes a double burden. The result is the fundamental psychological experience of impoverishment, which is loss of a sense of the value of the self, or, in the language used above, the loss of a positive emotional investment in the person taken as a whole.

Poverty is implied in the ascription of a denigrated identity. The essential meaning of poverty in the context of modernity is the loss of a sense of the value of our original impulse to shape a life and to be a creative force in doing so. It is not the things we lack, but the capacity to invest those things, and the life they express, with a special meaning linked to the "unique presence of being" we refer to as the self (Bollas 1989). Because of its connection to identity and to a concretely defined way of life, poverty is about need and access to the things we need.

## Need and identity

Using the notion of identity to define poverty has obvious advantages and equally obvious disadvantages. The advantages stem from the fact that the needs associated with individual identity are genuine needs; they are requirements of life and not mere preferences. To be sure, they are requirements of an individual way of life, one suited to a particular person with a particular history, character, interests, and abilities. They are nonetheless needs since a failure to satisfy them means an inability to continue on with a life that has substantial meaning. This failure is a real loss, and is attended by a real sense of impoverishment.

Developing, having, and expressing an identity are the essential elements in the investment of meaning in a way of life. So far as poverty refers to the inability to lead a way of life of a particular kind, it is natural to expect that the concept of identity will play a part, since it simply refers to an investment in a way of life. Our identification with our way of life means that we have made this investment. In thinking about poverty, emphasis on identity can lead us to consider poverty as the loss of an established identity. But, it can also lead us to consider poverty the original failure to develop such an identity.

To summarize what we have said so far: in a world of individuals, where a special value is invested in the process of self-discovery and in the needs associated with that process and its outcome, to be unable to undertake such a process means failure to realize the prevailing ideal. This failure results in a kind of deprivation, which is deprivation of meaning in life. Concern for individual autonomy should, then, lead us to consider the conditions for forming an individual identity as an essential element in our conception of poverty, which means that we need to understand something about the nature and origin of individual identity if we are to develop a concept of poverty appropriate to a world of individual self-determination.

Individual identity binds together the elements of an individual way of life into a whole and invests that whole with a special significance. One language used to refer to the source of significance for a way of life, and to the force that integrates a life experience so far as it involves the individual and a specifically individual identity, is the language of the self (Kohut 1977). Identity, then, is the expression of the condition of having or being your self in a concretely lived life.

Identity, then, expresses the idea that freedom means self-determination. This means that freedom is not simply the absence of coercion by and submission to others, nor is it simply autonomy from the group. It is the investment of meaning in a way of life made possible where we are free from the coercion of others. The formation of an individual identity expresses our self-determination, which exists in and through the process of self-discovery made possible by freedom from already known needs. As identity, self-determination takes the form of a concrete, particular life. In the language of the capabilities idea, to have an identity is to know the beings and doings that make life express self-determination. The concept of individual identity refers to a set of beings and doings that take on significance not because they establish that we are human, but because they express the organization of a way of life around the ideal of self-determination, and make that ideal real as the shape of a particular life.

## Work and identity

The idea of identity can help us understand better what it means to need and what it is that we need. What we need is to be active in determining what we do and who we are. When we consider the matter from the standpoint of doing as an expression of being, then we can begin to consider work as an expression of identity.

The link between work and identity suggests that work must have qualities suitable for it to realize freedom in being and doing. That is, work needs to be of a particular kind. This is not to say that identifications cannot be formed with work that fails to incorporate freedom, but only that when we do so our identity does not express self-determination, but the imposition of a way of life from outside. The question is not whether the individual identifies with his or her work, but whether that identification is suitable for realizing an ideal of self-determination in a concrete, particular life activity.

Whether identification with work realizes self-determination or not depends on qualities of the work. Understanding what these qualities are is the vital element in developing a concept of work suitable to the individual, a concept of the assets the individual needs if he or she is to be able to do such work, and therefore also a concept of poverty as the absence of those assets and thus the inability to do work that makes doing an expression of being. Following Winnicott, we will use the term creativity to refer to the essential element in a way of life in which doing is the expression of being. Creativity in work is then the quality that makes work appropriate to individual self-determination, and it is the capacity to do not merely work, and not merely remunerative work, but creative work that assures we are not poor. To understand better what this means, in Chapter 6 we consider the concept of creativity and creative living more closely. We then turn to the matter of work to see how a concept of creative work can be shaped and then applied to the problem of poverty.

# 6    Creativity and freedom

## Introduction

In Chapter 5, we considered the importance of the ideas of will, self, and identity. We suggest that the idea of will links what we do in the world to a creative act originating in the mind, which is the activity of imagining a world, or of conceiving an idea of a world, as it might be. The link between will and imaginative construction makes creativity a central element in our conception of work and its relation to freedom. We turn now to a fuller discussion of creativity so that its implications for work and poverty will become clearer.

A natural point of departure for doing so might lie in the common quality of work and creativity, which is that they are meant to produce something. Indeed, the term creativity is simply an extension of the term "to create", which is something we imagine that working will also accomplish, if not always in the same sense. Yet, even though the two activities are linked in this way, we will begin not with the production of something, but with the prior mental act, which is the conception of what might be produced. Creativity begins not in the hands but in the mind, which means that all creativity in conduct, including creativity in work, begins with creative thinking, or at least with the creative mental process.

## Thinking without presuppositions

Creativity in thinking refers to that quality of thinking that takes it out of already known channels. Creative thinking is thinking unconstrained by predetermined conclusions.[1] The ability to think creatively understood in this sense is not the property of a special group of people we judge creative in the usual sense: artists and writers, for example. Rather, creativity is an orientation to the world. In considering creativity this

---

[1] For a discussion of this idea in Hegel's philosophy, see Maker (1994).

way, we follow Winnicott's lead, since he considers creativity not as something to be applied exclusively, or even primarily, to a specific range of human endeavor.

You will agree that if someone is engaged in artistic creation, we hope he or she can call on some special talent. But for creative living we need no special talent. (Winnicott 1986: 44)

For Winnicott, creative living is to be understood in juxtaposition to its opposite, which is reactive living.

It is possible to show that in some people at certain times the activities that indicate that the person is alive are simply reactions to stimuli. Withdraw the stimuli and the individual has no life. (1986: 39)

Another term Winnicott uses for reactive living is compliance. The opposite of creativity is adapting how we think and how we live to the already known and previously approved, to follow lines of thought already laid out for us.

Its lack of constraint by what is already determined does not mean that creative thinking must always arrive at a new conclusion, and thus that it must reject what is already thought and known. Assuming that it must eventuate in something new is another false start in our thinking about creativity. What distinguishes creative thinking is not that by it we arrive at something new, but that by it we know something anew. This means that what we come to know is known by us in a different sense. It is not known to be true because it carries the weight of authority, but because we have thought our way to it. Since the thinking with which we are concerned here is unconstrained by prior conclusions, we can also call it thinking set free of external determination. In this sense, creativity and freedom refer to the same phenomenon. Thus, we can say that freedom in thought and conduct does not require us to reject what is and has been, though it might lead us in that direction.

Since the primary characteristic of creativity is its rejection of predetermination, creativity has a special relation to modern society (see Maker 1994: ch. 1). This is not to say that the individual can only be creative in those societies that consider themselves modern, or that all or most of those living in self-styled modern societies are creative in thought and conduct. Rather, it is to say that a part, perhaps the most important part, of the idea of modernity is its rejection of predetermination of thought and conduct in custom and tradition.

Since creativity rejects predetermination, it involves negation and therefore destruction. Destruction is the negative moment of creativity. Thus, for Picasso, a picture is a "sum of destructions," which means that for him creation is a sum of destructions. This connection of creation to destruction does not, of course, mean that nothing is produced. On the contrary, in the final product "nothing is lost."[2] We can say that destruction is uncreative when the creative capacity is itself the object to be destroyed. This type of destruction seeks to take from others what has been taken from the self: its vitality or sense of aliveness. Thus, Arthur Hyatt-Williams, referring to a person who was unable to cope with and contain his destructive impulse, notes that he "used to say of creative projects put to him, 'I will kill it! I will kill it stone dead'" (1998: 36).

What enables us to set aside what has been given to us and suspend the known world? We will argue that the answer to this question involves a specific relation between two different mental processes, which are sometimes thought of as two different parts of the mind. Put another way, we will argue that creative thinking involves the opening of a channel of a special kind between the conscious and unconscious, one in which neither dimension of mental functioning overwhelms the other.[3] These two parts of the mind represent thinking as we usually imagine it, and the suspension of thinking, or the process of not thinking, as we will refer to it. We will understand not thinking as an active process, and as the starting point of creative thinking. We will also emphasize the capacity to dwell in the mind (or inner world) as the essence of creative thinking. What gets in the way of creative thinking is an inability to dwell in the mind, possibly resulting from a fear of what we will find there.

Because it does not focus specifically on what is new, the way of using the term creativity suggested here might seem idiosyncratic. It does, nonetheless, incorporate something essential in what it means to create. Thus, the *Oxford English Dictionary* defines the verb "to create" with reference to a divine agent as "to bring into being, cause to exist" and includes in the definition the idea that to create is "to produce where nothing was before" (2nd edition, 1989). The idea of producing something out of nothing is what we have in mind by thinking without presupposition. This means that thinking does not simply recall what it has already thought, but produces something, an idea, let us say, of which it was not already aware. For the mind engaged in this creative

---

[2] From Ghiselin (1952: 56), quoted in Bruner (1962: 27).

[3] Kubie (1958) suggests we consider creativity not as a relationship between conscious and unconscious, but between unconscious and preconscious. There are good reasons for following him in this. In Chapter 7, we consider some of the issues involved in distinguishing between different modes of mental functioning. For the moment, we collapse all those that are not in awareness at a point in time under the heading "unconscious" which admittedly obscures the distinction Kubie emphasizes.

act, the product is new, though in the larger world of human experience it might already exist, having been conceived (created) by someone else. The link between someone who creates and the divine is well expressed by Winnicott when he notes how creativity involves "the retention throughout life of something that belongs properly to infant experience: the ability to create the world" (1986: 40). The ability to create the world is our ability not to take the world for granted, as something given to us without regard to our experience of ourselves as subjects. To be a subject means to be a source or origin, and thus to be creative. This ability originates in the infantile fantasy of creating its world with which Winnicott is particularly concerned.[4] The loss of this fantasy and of the creative capacity that goes with it destroys the feeling of aliveness that, for Winnicott, makes life worth living. Yet, to live creatively is not to live according to a delusion about the world: that it is our product and can be made to fit our wishes. The problem is to live creatively in a world we do not create or control. Finding this intermediate space, as Winnicott terms it, which is found between the givenness of things for us and the fantasy of omnipotence, is the task of creative living, and therefore of creative thinking.

One way in which creative thinking produces something from nothing is that it arrives at a state of knowing from a state of not knowing. Creative thinking is thinking that does not already know from the outset what it thinks. Another way of saying this is to say that creative thinking begins with not thinking.

### Not thinking

Larry Hirshberg, founding director of Nissan Design Incorporated, finds the locus of creativity in the "limbo space, that uncommitted, non-biased, and uncomfortable region in between zones of familiar knowledge" (Hirshberg 1998: 83). To get into this space involves a specific act: the suspension of conscious control over thought. Put another way, creativity requires access to a part of the mind that operates according to rules different from those with which we are familiar in our conscious experience of thinking. Creativity entails "the holding of apparently disconnected, conflicting, overlapping, or even mutually exclusive thoughts in the mind simultaneously" (Hirshberg 1998: 22).

Unprecedented thinking expands the limits of what constitutes appropriate, responsible, reliable, and intelligent thought beyond the strictures of the scientific method. It engages the logical with the emotional, the scientific with the

---

[4] Consider also Kohut's emphasis on "grandiose fantasies of the self" (1986).

aesthetic. It requires reorientation and disorientation. It engages the instinctive creative capacities of the unschooled child and, like the child, uses the fruits of failure and play. . . . Creative activity . . . does not confine itself to inbounds play. It comes to life at the edges, whether by blurring, abrading, overlapping, or breaking through the partitions. (Hirshberg 1998: 24)

We do not find creative solutions to problems by a process of logical deduction, or by the rule-bound application of the "scientific method," although deduction and induction can play a part in stimulating the mind's creative capacities.

Creativity engages the unconscious dimension of mental functioning since, paradoxically, creative thinking requires suspension of thought processes, which is to say it requires not thinking. Thus, in attempting to solve a design problem, participants "were encouraged not to think about the subject for a while" (Hirshberg 1998: 83). In this connection, Hirshberg recounts an experience where his response to the failure of the group to solve a problem was to take the entire team to a movie. Shifting from the work situation and the attempt to grapple with the problem head-on to the movie theatre and the suspension of problem solving and reality testing, encouraged the members of the group to regress to more primitive levels of mental functioning. This regression is at the heart of the creative process. Indeed, without regression, creative thinking would not be possible, since regression opens up the channel to which we have referred.

As Hirshberg emphasizes, what stands in the way of creativity is premature closure.

Too many managers and executives see their primary roles as continually push-ing for clarity and bottom-line resolution. They assume that to run or end a meeting without a clear direction or resolution is to fail. Noncommitment to a point of view is considered an equivocation, a position of weakness. In fact, it is a highly challenging and brave state of mind to retain, requiring a secure sense of self and an awareness that real confidence lies outside any specific ideological position. (Hirshberg 1998: 82–83)

Living creatively means not knowing already what must be done and what must be thought. Living creatively means not taking the questions and their answers for granted.

### Destruction

Creative thinking, whether it creates something new or not, involves the mental destruction of what has been presupposed, or assumed to be already known. This mental destruction is exemplified by Hirshberg's account of his group's efforts to design a child's chair. No progress was made in the design process until someone asked the question: what is a child? Only by asking this question could the group arrive at the thought that they could not design a child's chair because they did not know what a child is. Thus, the presumption that they knew what a child is stood in the way of their coming to know what a child is and what sort of chair would fit a child. Then, to create a child's chair, they must first destroy the (fixed or given) idea of a child with which they began.

Destruction of what we know leaves us in a state of not knowing. We lose that sense of security we have so far as we take the world for granted. Tolerating uncertainty is, then, vital to the creative process; and the inability to tolerate uncertainty (or the fear of it) impedes creativity.[5] What results from suspending what we know is formlessness or uninte-gration, which Winnicott considers the location of creativity. This is also the "area of freedom" (Eigen 1996: ch. 7). It would seem, then, that creativity arises out of unintegration, which is its source. Yet, while unintegration may be an essential moment of creativity, it cannot be the whole of it, since it does not in itself produce anything. Indeed, not thinking can have the most destructive consequences.

We have so far emphasized the link between creativity and not thinking, which might be taken to imply that thinking is opposed to creativity. This need not, however, be the case. Much depends on how we understand thinking, and especially how we understand what can be accomplished by it. Clearly, creativity cannot simply refer to the absence of thinking, even if that absence makes creativity possible. Rather, cre-ativity should be understood first as an opening of a channel between thinking and not thinking so that the product of not thinking can be thought. In creative living, before thinking there is not thinking, and before acting there is thinking. Allowing the product of not thinking to be thought is not, however, simply a matter of passively receiving the unthought into the conscious mind. Thinking also acts on the material not thinking makes available to it by transforming that material in ways that are essential if the product is to express a creative process. Let us consider, then, how thinking might be a creative act.

To do so let us consider further the link between creativity and synthesis.

Synthesis is the principal impulse of the act of creation. In a world obsessed with analysis, with the taking apart of things, creativity is the impulse to inte-grate, unify, and bring together. It tolerates (and at the early stages even prefers)

---

[5] French and Simpson (1999) emphasize the importance of tolerating not knowing in organizations.

higher levels of disorder and disintegration so that it can reorder at newer and higher levels of integration. (Hirshberg 1996: 25)

Creativity, then, is the reordering of experience that has integration rather than novelty as its end, though, of course, the resulting integration may be new to others as it certainly is to the individual involved in thinking creatively (Bruner 1962: 22). If to create is to bring form out of formlessness, integration out of unintegration, this should tell us something about what it is we create when we think and live creatively.

## Creativity and autonomy

While creativity does not imply that we will produce something new, it is clear that the creative stance fosters change.[6] The link to change suggests an important link between creativity and the attitude toward living peculiar to modern society. That attitude differs sharply from the orientation typical in premodern settings, where there is a need to protect existing ways of life and, more importantly, to protect the core animating idea in traditional society: that ways of life are predetermined. Thus, the issue of change is not so much about whether things are different or not, but whether they are predetermined and already known, or indeterminate and unknown.

Consider, as an example, the account offered by the historian Tzvetan Todorov of Aztec civilization at the moment of its encounter with Cortez (Todorov 1984: 66):

The whole history of the Aztecs, as it is narrated in their own chronicles, consists of realizations of anterior prophecies, as if the event could not occur unless it has been previously announced: departure from a place of origin, choice of a new settlement, victory or defeat. Here only what has already been Word can become Act.

It is not so much a matter of whether anything new happens in traditional societies, but of whether anything that happens is allowed to be new. This contrasts sharply with the habit of mind in the modern world, which insists on novelty even where an event is clearly an example of repetition rather than innovation.

The assumption of change expresses a wish as much as it describes an experience: the individual's wish to remake the world as his or her own product, an expression of his or her self in a form suited to his or her needs. This is a part of the wish that the world can be made new. We can express this idea by noting that remaking the world is no longer God's

---

[6] For a fuller discussion of creativity and change, see Levine (1999b).

work, but man's. More specifically, it is the work of the individual, and of each individual.

It may seem odd to raise change to the level of principle, as modernity seems to do. Yet, a purpose may lurk hidden in the impulse to reject all that is and has been, in the insistence on reinventing the world not only for each generation but also for each member of each generation. What might this something be? The German philosopher G. W. F. Hegel emphasizes freedom and its realization in ways of life and social institutions. Thus, modernity instantiates the "norm of freedom" into social institutions. Karl Marx sees in modernity an escape from the rigid and fixed givens of premodern existence. He sees in it an opportunity for what one of his students describes as liberation of "the human capacity and drive for development" (Berman 1982: 94, see also 127). For Hegel and Marx, the significance of change derives from its connection to freedom. This expresses an understanding of premodern, or traditional, society as one in which the member adopts a predetermined role, and in so doing adapts to, or complies with, given social meanings. The value now placed on change makes it possible for the individual to break free from the constraints that define the member. Change destroys the taken-for-grantedness of life. As a result, a life is not simply something we live, but also something we create, and in so doing we create ourselves. This creative act is the central significance of the idea of human development.

In the modern world, change and difference are not simply there for their own sake, but are the needed basis for us to be our selves. After all, if we are not different, then we cannot be ourselves but must be someone else: possibly a corporate or communal self rather than an individual. Modernity attacks the corporate self in the name of Erikson's "freedom of opportunities yet undetermined" (1964: 161–162). This is the freedom for each of us to shape a life and identity uniquely suited to us, one we do not know, and others do not know for us, until we find it for ourselves. This notion of identity formation differs markedly from that associated with premodern or traditional society, in which who we are is predetermined, and our ways of life are shaped for us.

The ideas of change and difference, then, are a part of the idea that persons can be separate (different and unique) units in the world. Modernity fosters the unit status of the individual, the emergent structure of a self, and of the self-boundaries that establish a world of different individual selves. These boundaries are not primarily physical, but emotional, which is to say that the salience of the physical boundaries lies in the way they also establish the separateness of the individual as this particular, unique person. The aspiration of the individual to "be real," which includes establishing the reality of the self in relations with that which is not-self (including especially other selves), is an aspiration to establish and maintain self-boundaries, not simply as a physical matter, but also psychologically. The idea of self-boundaries is reflected in self-integration, which unites the different aspects and dimensions of the self in a way that can secure the difference between what is self and what is not. Thus, it is self-integration that makes difference vitally important, since difference is the self's other side (Freedman 1980).

The importance of difference suggests one reason change looms so large in our way of characterizing what is modern. After all, to change means to become different, so it is through change that we establish difference. In this sense, change and difference are two ways of talking about the same thing: the emergence of the individual as the central ideal of social organization.

Change and difference involve reorganizing society around rule by the individual subject: property owner and citizen. In principle, decisions by consumers determine the use of economic resources, and decisions by citizens determine use of political power and public resources.[7] This identifies what many would consider the defining feature of modern society: the emergence of the autonomous individual, disembedded from the community, acting on his or her own, and for him or herself. The notions of property owner and citizen capture the emergence of the individual in the different spheres of economy and polity. Modernity, then, incorporates emancipation of the individual from the tradition-bound community. The separation, or disembedding (Polanyi 1957a), of the individual from the (traditional) community leads to a turning inward with an increased emphasis on private (or self) interest.

## Creativity and work

If we are to apply the term creativity to conduct, and especially to work, we cannot assume to know ahead of time what work will produce. Yet, we may still want to know something about the movement from conceiving to producing, from thinking to work understood as an activity aimed at making what we think become a reality for others. To conceive something is to produce an idea; to produce something more than an idea that remains in our minds, we must do more than conceive, we must also work to create our conception outside our minds. This is work as creative activity.

---

[7] We say "in principle" here. To organize political and economic life around the legal status of equal citizenship and property right does not guarantee that vital decisions are made by consumers or citizens.

The simplest way to link creativity to work is simply to note that creative thinking is a necessary, though not sufficient, condition for creative work. What is required over and above thinking and conceiving? One answer to this question emphasizes the element of skill. Then, what is needed for creative work is a particular capability to do something (skill), and the opportunity to do it (access to the necessary means and materials).

Using the term skill in this way restricts it to productive activity that expresses the prior mental activity of creative thinking. This aspect of skill is expressed in the connection between skill and expertise. Skill involves having a specific expertise. The term expertise also suggests how skill is linked to training; it is not something we are born with, though without sufficient talent we may never become skilled no matter how much training we have. Skill, then, is "expertise that comes from training" (*Webster's New World Dictionary*, Third College Edition). Even this, however, is not enough to define a skill, since the element of the capacity to do something is missing. Thus, we may have expertise in a subject matter by merit of having acquired broad knowledge of it, but this does not mean we have a skill, since it does not mean that we can do anything with our knowledge. To have a skill means to be able to do something with our knowledge.

The term skill is sometimes used to refer to the capacity to do something spontaneously (Argyris 1990: 20–21). This expresses the difference between the knowing linked to a skill and the knowing we link to following instructions. The former is a kind of knowing embedded in the unconscious mind as an ability we can call on in place of externally provided instruction. Because of this internalization, a skill is also an ability we have, and do not need to relearn each time we need to accomplish the task to which it is applied. When we act automatically and spontaneously, we express our freedom from rules and procedures that we must follow; we express our capacity to make our doing an expression of our being rather than an act of compliance with external authority.

We will find the archetype for this notion of skill in physical abilities such as the ability to ride a bicycle or play tennis. Here, skill refers to the ability of the mind to control the body without thinking about it, and without being aware of how this control is exerted. Yet, contrary to the description offered by Argyris, even these skills involve thinking and being aware of what we are doing. Part of having a skill is knowing how to make adjustments, when to apply what technique and when techniques do not apply, and how to correct our mistakes, all of which involve thinking about what we are doing. To be sure, the thinking about what we are doing associated with skill differs from the thinking about doing required by those who do not have the skill. This does not mean, however, that those who are skillful do not think about what they are doing, even though certain aspects of skillful activity take place outside of awareness. The necessity that we think about what we are doing when we are exercising a skill clearly distinguishes the exercise of skill from conduct driven by instinct or impulse. The use of a skill is not impulsive or instinctive, it is not altogether unconscious, but combines the conscious and unconscious aspects of mental activity in a particular way. In this sense, it is a specific way of uniting being and doing. We call on our skills when what needs to be done is not predetermined and cannot be reduced to a set of rules. Because of this, skill incorporates our creative capacities.

## Work and reality

Winnicott speaks of creative living in a very broad sense, one that does not restrict the application of the term creativity to work narrowly conceived as activity that produces a product, but includes all of what we do in the outside world that arises from an internal source and through which doing expresses being. Clearly, this use of the term creativity may include certain kinds of work while excluding others, and may also include activities we would not normally refer to as work. We might, of course, simply equate doing with work, and then divide work into that which is creative, expresses being, and that which is not creative. Using the term work in this broad sense extends it well beyond the limits of the kind of work normally considered in political economy. Whether work taken in this broader sense is creative or not does not depend on whether it is paid or whether its product takes on economic significance.

Work takes on an economic significance not according to whether it is or is not creative, but according to whether it does or does not have a particular kind of value for others. More specifically, work takes on economic significance when its product is for others, and is valued by them because it is of use to them. Work takes on economic significance when it enters into a universal interchange rather than being restricted to the sphere of personal experience and personal life. Thus, we can distinguish not only between work that is or is not creative, but also between work that eventuates in a product that is or is not of value for others.

Our emphasis on whether work is or is not creative tends to make poverty the inability to do creative work rather than the inability to do work whose product takes on value, and therefore significance, for others. A link between the two can be drawn, however, if we consider what makes work and its product real for the worker, and therefore what forges a link between the internal and the external worlds. Since forging that link is what we mean by doing, and therefore by work, it is clear that for being to be expressed it must take on reality for others, which is what work does when its product is for others. The special significance work's product takes on when it proves itself to have economic value is only one way in which work's product can demonstrate that it has significance in the outside world, but it is clearly an important way for work's product to prove that it is real in the sense that it exists outside the confines of the worker's subjective- or self-experience.

# 7    Work and freedom

## Work

In a setting where the classical economist's notion of subsistence applies, to be poor means to be unable to lead a life appropriate to a defined social position. Occupying such a position carries the meaning of existing for others, specifically for the community. If we use the term poverty to characterize those who lack something vital for living, in this setting poverty refers to the lack of a vital connection to the community. The poor are those who have been excluded from the community, or they are those whose community has somehow failed.

As we have suggested, this idea becomes difficult to apply where we deal not with members of a community, but with individuals, not with need defined by social position, but with individual need. Here, if poverty refers to a lack, it cannot be the older connection with the community that has been lost. Rather than referring to the failure of the connection with community, poverty now refers to a failure in the shaping or maintaining of an individual identity. While this identity may incorporate attachment to a group, this attachment is chosen rather than ascribed, and the individual seeks the group not to find an identity, but to express and realize it.

Associated with individual identity are a set of appropriate beings and doings. Focusing for the moment on doings, we can consider poverty the inability to make what we do in life an expression of our individual identity. This leads us to ask the following question: what sorts of doings are expressive of individual identity? This is a large question, and our concern is only with a part of it, specifically, that part that has to do with work. Work is, of course, something that we do, and, indeed, among the terms we use to speak about doings, work is of special importance. We can reformulate our question with respect to this particular form of doing: what sorts of work express individual identity? The answer to this question will also help us answer the question: what does it mean to be poor in a modern society?

The link between individual identity and work is also a link between freedom and work. The element of freedom in work has most often been formulated in the language of choice, especially choice of vocation. And, indeed, the opportunity to make choices about what we will do in life is a vital part of shaping and expressing individual identity. But, for what we do to express our autonomy, more is needed than choice. The doing chosen must be a vehicle through which an individual can express and realize his or her freedom. It is this embedding of freedom in doing that we will emphasize here. Our question about poverty, then, becomes the question: What kind of doing, or, more specifically, what kind of work, is appropriate to individual freedom (Hegel 1821: 128–129)?

We may begin to answer this question by noting that, in premodern settings, and often in the modern world, there is an at least tacitly assumed inconsistency between work and freedom. Thus, freedom is often taken to mean freedom from work, leisure and work relating as freedom and unfreedom. It would follow, then, that in such societies, free persons are those who do not work, but do things other than work. This means that those who work are not free, which is to say that they must be poor since they lack the opportunity, and possibly the capability, to make doing an expression of freedom.

This conclusion holds even where the worker is legally free in so far as his freedom does not extend to a way of life appropriate to a free person. He must work, and he must survive on his subsistence. His freedom therefore is not real in the sense that it remains external to his way of living. Marx imagines that capitalist development, by dramatically enhancing the productivity of labor, will ultimately make work unnecessary, and therefore establish what he refers to as the material conditions for freeing the worker, which is to say freeing him from the need to work. Thus, for Marx, work remains the antithesis of freedom; freedom means freedom from work (see Chapter 2). Why this conflict between work and freedom? And, if freedom means freedom from work, what does a free person do in life? To answer this question, we need to consider more closely what we mean by work, or, what it is we do when we work.

One answer to the question of what is it to work treats work as an essentially physical act, as Marx does when he distinguishes work from labor. Here, however, we will not use the term in this restrictive way, but rather to capture something of the significance Marx invests in the term labor. To clarify where this use of the term might lead us, we might begin with Marx's own, admittedly somewhat ambiguous, treatment of the idea of labor.

Marx begins by defining labor as an interchange between man and nature in which man acts as one of nature's own elements; man "opposes himself to nature as one of her own forces" ([1867]/1967: 177). The ambiguity in usage is already apparent here, since man both opposes nature and exists within it as one of nature's own forces. Marx seems to be aware of this ambiguity when he notes that this notion of labor, or work, in our terms, only applies to "those primitive instinctive forms of labour that remind us of the mere animal" (178). Marx does not concern himself with this form of labor, but only with that labor that appears "in a form that stamps it as exclusively human" (178). Indeed, it becomes clear enough that labor, as Marx goes on to conceive it, does not represent man within nature as one of nature's own elements working on nature, but man existing in a setting not offered anywhere by nature, neither acting as a force of nature nor acting on materials provided by nature. In Marx's depiction of the labor process, labor works only with materials produced by labor and using implements, especially machinery, produced not by nature but by man's own laboring. Marx refers to this new activity of laboring as labor's "exclusively human" form. This exclusively human form of labor is what we will mean by work.

What do we know about the human form of labor, or work? According to Marx, what gives labor its exclusively human form is that, at its end, "we get a result that already existed in the imagination of the labourer at its commencement" (178). Based on this discussion, we can extract from Marx a general statement of the meaning of work (or labor, in Marx's usage), which is also the meaning we will apply in our discussion of the problem of work and freedom. We will take it that work is the mediating term between an idea and its realization. Put another way, work is the active moment in a process of conception, where conception means both "to form or develop in the mind," and to "cause to begin life" (*Webster's New World Dictionary*, Third College Edition).

At this point, it would seem that work is a creative act that unifies subject (imagination) and object (product). Yet, as we know, this idea of work bears little resemblance to the process Marx goes on to explore in great detail in his writing on political economy. The labor that Marx explores there is not an activity in which the laborer's imagination plays any significant role. Rather than uniting subject and object in work, the labor Marx describes for us tears the two apart, making the worker not the subject of his laboring, but only another object in the process whose subject stands outside.

Marx goes on to note this, adding another ambiguity to his discussion of the labor process. He tells us that, in laboring, the worker "realizes a purpose of his own that gives the law to his modus operandi, and to which he must subordinate his will." For this subordination of will to take effect, the "workman must be steadily in consonance with his purpose," and give the work his "close attention." It follows, according to Marx, that the "less he is attracted by the nature of the work, and the mode in which it is carried on, and the less, therefore, he enjoys it as something which gives play to his bodily and mental powers, the more close his attention is forced to be" (178). Now, Marx has come close to reversing his original characterization of work as an imaginative act made real, turning it instead into an activity alien to the worker's imagination and subjectivity. And, clearly, this is the notion of work that takes center stage as Marx's description of labor in the setting of a modern economy develops. Here, it seems, however, that those aspects of work that make it alien to the worker as subject develop not because of the system of ownership of the means of production, but directly out of the nature of the labor that, according to Marx, bears an "exclusively human" stamp.

The ambiguity introduced by Marx into his conception of work is clear enough when we consider that he both defines work as the mediating term between idea and reality, and insists that in working the worker does not exercise his mental powers. This means that, while the idea precedes work, and must be realized in it, having the idea and exercising it are not directly part of the activity of work. Because of this, it becomes possible to separate the idea from the worker and treat the worker as an object. According to Marx, capitalistic production introduces this separation by embedding the idea of the product not in the mind of the worker but in the system of machinery in relation to which the worker is not a subjective element, but nothing more than an appendage.

If we return for a moment to work as the activity whose purpose is to bring about the unity of subjective and objective, then the alienated labor Marx refers to at the end of his definition is not labor, but at best a deformation of labor. This deformation develops because of the suppression of will in work, since it is the presence of will that gives that process its subjective meaning, makes it the act of a subject, an act that incorporates freedom and self-determination. The problem, then, is to understand better the role of will in work. Marx tells us that work requires the suppression of will, which means that work requires that the worker suspend his subjective existence and treat himself as another implement in a purely objective process (one of nature's own forces). So, according to Marx, work both is and is not a creative act.

There is in this less of a contradiction than we might at first imagine, since what happens, according to Marx, is that the unity of subjective and objective in work is destroyed by the subordination of the labor process to the end of making a profit. Subordination of work to this goal leads to the separation of its moments, so that the idea realized through work (the product) is not the laborer's. Still, it seems clear from Marx's language that what sets the labor process apart from the original idea of a unity of subjective and objective is not its subordination to profit-making, but something Marx considers, at least in this context, intrinsic to labor itself, which is the demand for "close attention," a demand that requires that the worker suppress his will.

The problem Marx encounters in his discussion of the labor process is also the problem with which we will be concerned here: the relationship between work, creativity, and freedom. We will follow Marx in considering work (labor) a creative act rather than a natural process, the act through which subjective and objective are united. To do so, we cannot, however, follow Marx in his insistence that work means suppression of will, which would set work in opposition to freedom. When the worker's subjective being stands opposed to the demands of work and must, in that process, be suppressed, then his work stands opposed to his freedom and, for him, there can be nothing creative in it. Work of this kind may express the will of forces standing outside the worker, but it cannot be an act of will on the worker's part. By contrast, when work and the close attention to detail often involved in it are an expression of the worker's will, there need be no opposition between subjective and objective. In this case, the mobilization of will is the essential element in work, since work becomes an act of will by which all desires and needs unconnected to the creative act must be suspended so that the worker can devote himself to his work.

## The opposition between work and freedom

The assumed inconsistency between freedom and work so prominent in the writings of the classical economists derives from a specific conception of labor as mind-deadening activity that uses a person as if he or she were a mere animal. Thus, Marx, at least in his later writing, as we have seen, goes so far as to define labor as a natural interchange, even an animal function. Yet, in doing so he leaves aside the link between labor and freedom emphasized in his early writings, where he considers labor a characteristically human activity, and in this sense suggests that the ability to labor should be considered the human capability above all others. These two positions are not inherently inconsistent if we take into account that Marx has two different sorts of work in mind. The sort of activity he associated with labor in his economic writings is work that involves no element of the worker's person aside from his or her physical capacities, and minimal mental control over them. The sort of activity considered in his earlier writings involves the unity of mind and work, and thus engages the worker as the agent of his activity.

It can be said that only the second type of work incorporates the element of freedom. But, if this is the case, it would seem to imply an inconsistency between freedom and the economic organization of modern society, where, at least according to Marx, work produces the material basis for freedom by adopting a form, dehumanized labor, that is the antithesis of freedom.

This conclusion may, however, express not the intrinsic logic of a modern capitalistic economy, but the specific shape that economy took in the early stages of its development. If we drop the hypothesis that, under capitalism, work must give up its connection to freedom, we open up a possible solution to the problem of the meaning of poverty. Poverty could refer to a condition in which the only capacity the individual has is his or her physical being, so that work cannot incorporate the element of freedom. If we are to understand poverty as the lack of freedom, we must, then, understand the way in which freedom is or is not incorporated into work.

Here, the connection of mind to work is the vital element. For work to incorporate freedom it must engage the worker's mind. Put another way, the worker must have knowledge and the ability to put that knowledge to practical use in doing something. He or she must have the ability to use his or her mind to direct activity that reshapes the external world.[1] Work that incorporates mind is what we referred to in the last chapter as skilled labor, so we can say that the incorporation of freedom into laboring and the use of skill in laboring are one and the same thing. To be without skill is to be unfree in your activity; and to be unfree in your activity is to be irrelevant to, or at least marginal in, society, and therefore poor. Then, if the destruction of skilled labor is the necessary basis for the production of wealth, as Marx insists it is, and if it establishes the foundation for freedom from want, freedom and unfreedom must be inextricably interconnected. But, if the destruction of skilled labor Marx observes at the beginning of capitalist development is only the destruction of the older skills appropriate to an older society, then we need not conclude that the material conditions for a free society demand that workers give up their freedom if they are to work.

---

[1] While this reshaping is often of the physical world, this is not a necessary condition for defining the kind of work under consideration here.

## Skills, creativity, and freedom

If skill represents the element of freedom in work, then freedom means (1) that the worker is the legal owner of his or her capacities, and (2) that the worker has a skill. If only those who work can be free, since only in work of a particular kind can we unify freedom with activity, then wealth cannot bestow freedom.

This conclusion will not seem so implausible if we consider it in relation to the idle rich, who may not be poor by standards of ownership of wealth, but whose lives may nonetheless be considered impoverished if all they do is consume goods or exhibit themselves as the owners of wealth. More specifically, if they do nothing that involves the use of their creative capacities, they can hardly be considered free no matter how much wealth they may have; and in being unfree they are impoverished, at least by the standards of a society organized around the ideal of freedom. The conclusion to draw from this is that the society of free persons is the society of those who work in a particular sense of the term. The poor are those who do not work in that way, regardless of the amount of wealth they may have accumulated. This does not prevent us from distinguishing between those who have wealth and those who do not, but it does imply that having wealth does not secure freedom.

It may not be obvious, however, why the element of skill in work is so important to the matters of freedom and poverty. What is it about skill that makes it the expression of human freedom, bearing in mind that historically not all of those who have a skill are legally free? To answer this question, we need to consider the unity of work and mind, which is to say skill, more closely.

A skill is an acquired capacity to do something in a particular way: skillfully. Acquiring and exercising a skill demands the integration of thinking and doing. To learn a skill, we must think about what we are doing. The link between skill and freedom requires that we cannot do what needs to be done by following a prescribed routine that can be registered in the mind as a fixed procedure. For the creative exercise of a skill, what has been termed "procedural learning," is not enough (on procedural learning, see Grigsby and Stevens 2000). There must be something more. We can think of this something more as the element of the unknown. Creativity in work means that what we do cannot be fully known to us before we do it. This element of the unknown in doing makes it a part of the experience of freedom. It is also the creative element in doing. That what we do is not already known makes what we do a creative act. The being appropriate to freedom is the being that makes creativity possible. If being implies acting on the basis of an internal rather than external principle of regulation, then the doing that arises out of being contains the element of creativity, and therefore freedom.

It is because of this element that, when we exercise a skill in work, we are not bored or alienated, but engaged. If by interest we refer to the significance that an object or activity has for the self, we can say of skilled work that it interests the worker. By contrast, unskilled labor does not engage the worker precisely because it is essentially routine, and the involvement of mind is kept to the minimum called for to direct simple physical movements. Thus, unskilled labor tends to be uninteresting, tedious, alienating.

Since skillful work engages our mind as the controlling element, it cannot be directed from outside. This gives us an important clue to the link between skilled work and freedom. Whether the skilled worker is legally free or not, his activity contains an element of freedom, since in the act of working he is the controlling force. On the other side, even if the unskilled worker is legally free, his activity lacks the element of freedom since he is not the controlling force, and he is therefore unfree.

The link between skill and the creative element in work makes skill an intrinsic, and in this sense objective, quality of certain kinds of work and not something we can attribute to work based on the state of demand for it or the level of remuneration it can command. That work is poorly paid, or not paid at all, does not bear on our judgment of whether it requires the exercise of skill. The link between skill and creativity can, of course, be a matter of degree, and different types of work, or even the same type of work done under different conditions, can afford the opportunity for the exercise of the human creative capacity to different degrees. Since the exercise of skill requires that the work not be predetermined for the worker, the context of work also comes into play. The less discretion the worker has in how he or she works, the less that work offers an opportunity for creativity, and the less skill, in this sense of the term, is involved.

### Work, character, and authority

In a traditional society, the kind of work the individual does, if any, depends not on acquired qualities of character, but on ascribed characteristics. If we think of the matter in the language of right, we can say that it is a matter not of the individual's right to pursue a self-chosen vocation, but of the individual's birthright to occupy an already determined position in a more or less fixed social division of labor and social hierarchy. This is not to say that work and character have no connections in traditional societies. The adaptation of one to the other proceeds, however, primarily from the demands of type of work and ascribed social position to character, so that the latter must be molded to suit the former.

The more an economy is organized along modern lines, the less well this system works (Gellner 1983). This is in part because the traditional system does not assure the flexibility needed to adapt work to changing requirements of developing technology and a developing system of needs. It is also because the underlying principle of a modern economy – individual right – conflicts with the idea of ascription demanded to provide normative standing to the older system of work allocation. Once we begin to consider the allocation of work a matter of individual choice, we also begin to move away from the older idea and to take into account the fit between work and character as a necessary element in the division of labor. This fit is no longer essentially a matter of assuring that members of status groups, classes, and guilds have the character appropriate to their assigned activities, but more and more a matter of the individual finding a vocation that fits his or her character.

Now, each individual must find a type of work with an intrinsic meaning appropriate to his or her character. The more we consider individual character not simply as a means to adapt the individual to work and social position, the less we can justify insisting that individuals give up vital qualities of personhood in order to work. Rather, work should be a setting in which qualities of personhood can find expression. As a result, there develops within the workplace a struggle between two principles: the principle that the worker's character should be adapted to the demands of work, and the principle that the individual should be able to choose a vocation that fits his or her character.

Larry Hirschhorn has described this struggle in the language of psychological presence, arguing that in what he refers to as the "postmodern" workplace, which is what we have referred to as the modern work setting, the worker must be "psychologically present" (Hirschhorn 1997). The point that Hirschhorn makes is that when work evolves to incorporate discretion, and especially creativity, when it is no longer routinized and determined by objective rules given independently of the worker, then work engages the worker's self. This engagement of self implies that the self must be present during work if the work is to be done well.

If we consider this proposition in relation to the distinction between personal and professional selves, it suggests we consider how that distinction develops and applies where work incorporates the element of human creativity.[2] For work to incorporate that element it must engage the worker, including aspects of the worker's character. The worker's character must be suited to the kind of work he or she does. For example, an individual with a scientific temperament will be better suited to work in a laboratory than will an individual with no such inclination. The worker must be personally engaged in the work; it must have an intrinsic meaning for him or her, if it is to be done well.

The connection of work to character has implications, as Hirschhorn goes on to suggest, for authority in the workplace. The authority system appropriate to alienated labor differs from an authority system appropriate to work that engages the individual's self, expresses his or her character and creative capability. The difference leads not in the direction of democratization of the workplace and the overthrow of authority, but in the direction of establishing an appropriate relationship between authority and skill. This follows from the necessity that work have a creative element, since for it to have that element, the worker doing it must have a significant degree of discretion over what he or she does; and for there to be discretion, there must be authority.

The conclusion we would draw from this is that a workplace suited to creative work is one in which the worker is psychologically present, is able to express the close connection between work and character, and has authority over his or her work. It follows that in this setting, authority follows skill, and is simply a necessary aspect of a work setting in which skill can be exercised. Once, however, we link authority to skill, we also set limits on authority, since authority is also limited by skill, by the limits of the skill of the individual worker, and by the presence of other workers with different skills. The system of skill and expertise grounds a system of authority over work, one that allows adequate authority to the individual worker for him or her to exercise skill and work creatively.

## Exclusion

Given the association between skills and freedom, those who are poor are so because they have failed to acquire a skill, or because, having acquired a skill, they cannot find employment offering the opportunity to exercise it. We begin with the first possibility.

The question of poverty is first the question: What stands in the way of the acquisition of skill? Since skills are acquired by a training process, we are less inclined to treat their absence as an expression of an original

---

[2] In fact, Hirschhorn tends to reject this distinction.

lack, but to see it instead as the result of the failure of access to a needed training. Thus, the link between freedom and skill overthrows the link between freedom and attributes of birth. Because of this, it also overthrows the idea that freedom is a natural attribute, that we are born free or born with innate rights. Thus, if freedom is not a birthright of the ruling classes because of who they are (and what position they were born into), neither is it a birthright of all who were born into the appropriate species.[3] If freedom is not a birthright, then it must be attained, and some will likely fail to do so. What sorts of factors might account for failure?

Much depends on how we conceive the initial endowment required for learning a skill, and the process by which a skill is learned. Difficulties begin with the distinction between having some skill, whatever it might be, and acquiring any particular skill. It is one thing to say that, at birth, all, or almost all, human beings have the assets required to develop *some* skill to at least some degree, but it is another matter to suggest that human beings are all born with the assets required to develop *all* skills. Few would insist on the second proposition, which effectively dismisses any requirement that we have some talent in a particular area if we are to develop the relevant skill.

The more talent required to develop a skill, the more appropriate it is to exclude some who wish to learn the skill from the opportunity to do so. This means that access to particular skills is not available to all, but only to those who can demonstrate that they have the requisite talent. Clearly, it is an implication of this conclusion that those who have no talent of any kind relevant to developing a skill cannot do so, will likely be excluded from access to the needed training, and will as a result find their participation in society sharply limited.

To get to this result, we must first have an appropriate test, and however straightforward testing skills might be, the same cannot be said for testing talents before they have had the chance to develop into skills. We can solve the problem of judging talent in two ways. The first is by assuming that certain sorts of people have certain talents and others do not. That is, assuming that talent is innate, we can make the further assumption that possession of the talent expresses itself somehow in the individual's natural endowment. This procedure justifies limiting access to training on the grounds of natural characteristics such as gender and race that are assumed to be markers for relevant talents.

---

[3] Treating freedom as something other than a birthright need not limit what rights we have, though it may limit our conception of who has the capacity to act on the basis of right (see Levine 2001: ch. 4).

We can, however, only keep this procedure secure by assuring that those who do not fall into the appropriate groups are not given the opportunity to discover whether they do indeed have talent, which we do by barring them from admission to training programs. Yet, the fact that the skill is evidently the result of training tends to suggest that those lacking it might do so because they do not have the training, and this challenges the assumption that the matter of who does or does not have the talent to acquire a skill can reasonably be settled by considering physical characteristics not in any obvious way linked to doing what the skill enables one to do.

When we settle the matter of who can or cannot acquire a skill by appeal to *a priori* considerations, especially attributes of birth, we assure that poverty will also be judged an *a priori* condition, or the expression of such a condition. Indeed, this is the point. Here, we make poverty and freedom expressions not of what we can do, but of who we are assumed, and assume ourselves, to be.

If we reject the idea of freedom as a birthright, then, so far as the matter of skill is concerned, it follows that we cannot know who does or does not have the relevant talent except by affording all the opportunity to exhibit that talent, which can only be done in a setting where the talent can express itself as a skill, in however rudimentary a way, which is part of what a modern educational system attempts to do. Those who cannot do biology well in school can be judged lacking the talent needed to become doctors; those who cannot do math well can be judged lacking the talent needed to become engineers, and so on. Whatever else we might expect our schools to do, they must also provide a setting in which the presence of talent can be judged in practice rather than *a priori*. The test applied in this way may not be perfect, but it does embody the principle that talent is not ascribed on the basis of considerations other than the talent itself.

Still, some will fail not only at exhibiting talent for this or that skill, but also at exhibiting any talent whatever. And, some who seem to have the talent will never succeed in developing it into a skill, even if they are afforded the opportunity to do so. Affording all the opportunity does not assure that all will take advantage of it. While it may seem simple enough, at least in principle, to deal with poverty when it clearly results from limiting access to training so that a class of persons are excluded and thus must be poor, it is a more difficult matter to consider how some end up poor when their access is not restricted in this way. Are the poor poor because, even though they may have some talent, they cannot undergo the process that develops talent into skill? When we consider the answer to this question, we consider what is needed to learn a skill, and when we do so we will learn something important about the relationship between skill and freedom, since it is the capacity for autonomy that ultimately underlies the capacity to learn a skill.

One conclusion we can draw from this discussion is that when we consider poverty the loss of freedom and freedom the ability to exercise a skill, we define poverty as a developmental failure, the failure to develop a skill. Or, at least, we find that poverty not linked to trends in the economy and technology is an expression of failed development. This failure may result from external or from internal factors, and it is important to know which are primary. But, in either case, the matter of development is vital, and poverty refers to a condition of blocked development, or developmental failure.

## Skill and identity

Since having a skill does not assure the availability of employment utilizing that skill, acquiring a skill does not assure the unity of doing and freedom. Those who have a skill, but cannot exercise it, are also poor, but in a different way from those who cannot acquire a skill. We can speak of this difference in the language of identity. Acquiring and having a skill shapes a part of the individual's identity. Exercising the skill and maintaining a way of life appropriate to a person who exercises that skill express a vital aspect of individual identity. Loss of the opportunity to exercise skill because an appropriate job is unavailable means loss of identity. Then, doing can no longer express being, and the result is impoverishment in the sense in which the term is used here.

When we think about poverty in this way, poverty as identity deprivation and poverty as lack of skill lead us in the same direction. The link between poverty and deprivation of identity parallels the older subsistence-based notion of poverty defined within a moral order. Poverty in a moral order means lack of access to the subsistence appropriate to a position within that order. Subsistence is linked to identity as the means to secure a way of life appropriate to it. The links between poverty and identity in the two settings differ, however, first in that the modern setting incorporates the element of creativity in living, of doing as an expression of being in Winnicott's sense. They also differ because the source of the subsistence differs from the source of the employment needed to sustain a modern identity linked to a vocation. The former was a matter of duty and obligation, and the identity that the community sustained through its members as temporary carriers of a specific position and role was an identity the community was obligated to support for the member. In the modern world, where member gives way to individual, no such obligation exists. Whatever obligation may exist in the area of income support does not readily extend to the area of support for identity rooted in a vocation and the associated opportunity to exercise a skill. Thus, if we accept the link between poverty and the loss or absence of the opportunity to exercise a skill, poverty under the circumstances considered here results not from a failure of obligation, but from cyclical or secular trends in economic activity and in technology, trends that are, in part at least, an expression of human creativity. Poverty can result, then, not only for those who have no skill, but also for those who do. In a context of economic change, no assurance can be provided that skill will secure freedom from poverty. This conclusion may be modified, but it is not fundamentally overthrown, if the society offers income support to those whose skills are no longer needed, since this still leaves them without the opportunity for creative living so far as that requires the exercise of their skill.

It follows from the link between poverty, freedom, and skill that poverty cannot be eliminated or altogether avoided, especially in a technically dynamic society. This does not mean that nothing can be done to reduce or minimize the incidence of poverty. Nor does it mean that nothing can be done to limit the suffering of those who are poor. It does suggest, however, that we can only eliminate poverty if we either consider poverty something other than lack of freedom or treat freedom as exclusively an objective condition and not a matter of what the individual is capable of doing and being.

### Skill and income

Difficulties in reconciling subsistence-based ideas of poverty with the nature of a modern society have led us to consider poverty not as the failure to sustain a prescribed level of living, but as the failure to develop the ability to incorporate into life the specific sort of doing associated with creative living. This special sort of doing, when considered concretely as a particular activity, is the doing that demands access to and use of skill. Yet, while this alternative way of thinking about poverty does not emphasize income levels and living standards, there are links between skill and income. And, while in some ways a digression from our main concerns, it might be useful to review some of these links.

We might begin with the simple and well-known correlation between poverty levels defined in the usual way (Fisher 1997), and levels of education. Data collected by the US Census Bureau in 2002 suggest a strong correlation between poverty levels and levels of education as indicated in the Table 7.1:

Table 7.1. *Educational level and poverty*

| Educational level (both sexes, all ages) | Percent below poverty line | Percent of poor |
| --- | --- | --- |
| No High School Diploma | 22.3 | 38.9 |
| High School Diploma | 9.6 | 33.5 |
| Some College, no Bachelors Degree | 6.6 | 18 |
| Bachelors Degree or More | 3.3 | 9.6 |

*Note:* US Census Bureau, Current Population Survey, March 2002.

The data presented in the table strongly suggest that a substantial part of poverty as that is usually defined is explained by lack of education. This does not make education the causal factor, since access to education and ability to take advantage of the educational opportunities available must be taken into account. Still, the fact that 90 percent of the poor as traditionally defined lack a college degree, and that of those with a college degree only 3.3 percent are poor strongly supports the idea that poverty measured in the standard way expresses factors closely linked to those we have emphasized here.

We cannot assume any simple relationship between skill and education, though we can assume that jobs requiring more education are also jobs for which mental capacities are of predominant importance. Assuming that skill is correlated with the use of mental capacities, as suggested above, and therefore with education, it follows that the correlation between poverty measured by income and living standard is also correlated with poverty defined as the lack of a skill. This is not the whole story of poverty, nor is it the whole story of the link between poverty, income, and skill, but it is important.

The importance of the correlation between income and skill lies in the connection between individuation, and thus freedom, and the access to an adequate amount of wealth (see Levine 1995). Even if we cannot establish a meaningful level of wealth adequate to support individuation without taking into account the individual's identity and self-chosen way of life, we can insist that individuation and freedom do require wealth. As it turns out, the amount of wealth needed is highly variable. Yet, the poverty level as normally defined in statistical studies in the United States does, as its founder suggests, tell us how much is too little, even "if it is not possible to state unequivocally 'how much is enough,'" (something we can only know *a priori* in a traditional society).[4]

---

[4] Quoted in Fisher (1997).

### Poverty policy

Poverty may result from our lacking the capacity to be (in Winnicott's sense), so that instead of being, we can only react to stimuli. Or, poverty may result from our lacking the opportunity to make doing an expression of being. If we assume that all, or nearly all, humans are born with the potential to live creatively, to make doing an expression of being, then poverty means that this potential is somehow lost, or, if it is retained, it is not possible to exercise it. The problem of poverty is, then, the problem of the loss either of a capability or of an opportunity.

This conclusion bears on the formulation of policy aimed at dealing with poverty. If the goal of policy is to provide jobs without regard to the presence in them of the element of creativity in work, jobs which are, therefore, unsuitable to those with the capacity to make doing an expression of being, then the policy does not address the problem of poverty as we have defined it here. Similarly, if the goal of policy is to provide income, then policy does not even address the problem of poverty, which is that of creativity in work. This does not mean that providing jobs or income to those who have neither is bad policy, but only that it is not policy directed at the problem of poverty, except in the sense that it is hoped to eliminate poverty's most visible expressions and consequences. If we are really to address the problem of poverty, we must take on the problems of capability and opportunity.

While it can be said that the problem of opportunity has been a primary concern of social policy, especially during the last half of the twentieth century, the same cannot be said about the problem of capability. Indeed, the concern with opportunity has at times served as a way of avoiding the problem of capability. This avoidance is built into policy-making when it incorporates the idea that only external obstacles to creativity in living have meaning, and that, given opportunity, creativity will flourish. This assumes that no experience in life can impair, or even destroy, the original capacity for creative living. When policy aimed at the problem of opportunity contains this assumption, it both alleviates poverty and avoids dealing with the problem of poverty, which is a problem not only of doing, but also of being.

Freedom means little without creativity. Work without creativity is unfree regardless of the legal-institutional setting within which it takes place. Only work that allows expression of the creative impulse can be considered well suited to a free person; only such work is the doing that expresses freedom. In a moral order, work's end is not creative expression, but the fulfillment of duty to the community. The virtue of such work lies not in its connection to freedom, but in the way it expresses and confirms the primacy of the group and the member's aspiration to belong. Here, virtue means service. That the moral order cannot be a setting for freedom and human creativity means that any ideal organized around the norm of freedom and its expression in creative living must stand beyond the moral order.

None of this implies that beyond the moral order work has no value other than the experience it offers the worker for creative expression. Creative work can also be useful work. This is because creative work links the worker not only to an inner experience, but also to reality. Creative work binds creativity with adaptation to a world not of the worker's making. This world is the world of others, also seeking to live creatively in a world they do not create.

# 8    Work and satisfaction

A commonly stated motivation for economic policy is to benefit people's welfare, happiness, or satisfaction. We want to promote particular policies because of their beneficial impact on people's lives. Yet central aspects of conventional economic method seem to prejudge what makes people's lives go well. In the neoclassical conception, individuals choose goods and services to maximize utility subject to an income constraint, where income derives primarily from the sale of labor. Thus the goal of economic activity is consumption, which leads to higher utility. Consumption is constrained by income, so income and utility or satisfaction should be clearly related. Labor, on the other hand, is avoided, since it enters negatively into the utility function. Labor and leisure relate as negative to positive, the amount of work depending on a tradeoff between labor and leisure that is affected by the wage. Thus it is assumed that what makes life go well is income and consumption; what is to be avoided is labor. The amount of work performed depends on the amount of disutility that must be endured to derive income from the sale of labor.[1] To the extent we want to maximize welfare, we would want to reduce work and increase income and consumption.

With this answer to the question of what makes life go well, we also have a solution to the problem of defining and alleviating poverty. Poverty is lack of income – income being more concrete than an adequate level of utility – and the solution to poverty is to provide more income or a to provide a way to earn more of it. Work enters to the extent it can provide income. Thus, in one way of thinking about poverty, alleviation requires transfer payments, either within countries or among

---

[1] There are, however, some cases where this cannot be true. Volunteer work is undertaken without payment, which might lead some to classify it as a species of leisure. Similarly, different degrees of work must have different degrees of disutility, since some types of work can be more distasteful, routine, boring, repetitive, risky, and so on, than others. A worker on an offshore oilrig will need to be paid more than a typical construction worker. These wage differences, corresponding to different disutilities, are called compensating wage differentials. Yet despite these modifications to the basic idea, the main theory of work in neoclassical economics is to treat it as a disutility.

countries. In another approach, contrasted to the first as though they were opposites, poverty alleviation means making people work, no matter what sort of work is involved and – so it seems – at whatever cost to other aspects of life. Both approaches rely, however, on a similar concept of poverty, one that is underlined by the neoclassical approach to what makes a life go well. If this concept of what makes a life go well is found wanting, we are quite likely to have a different answer to what causes poverty and how to alleviate it. So theories of well-being and poverty are fundamentally related.

Utility is not a concept that people consciously employ. They do not say that what they are doing is to maximize utility. Yet few individuals would argue that they do not want to increase a near-synonym, such as happiness or satisfaction, interpreted appropriately. This allows us to ask whether the concentration on income as a source of satisfaction and work as a source of dissatisfaction is correct. To answer this question, we can turn to the literature in social psychology and sociology concerned with the determinants of happiness or satisfaction. Since this literature asks broader questions, and since it is concerned with the quality of life generally and not just its economic components, we can use it to see what features of life relate best to satisfaction and see how they relate to the economy.

### Methodological issues

"Since the mid-1960s . . . there have been literally thousands of studies (cross-sectional, cross-cultural, and historical) of the nature and sources of reported work, marital and life satisfaction" (Lane 1991: 435). In these studies, survey respondents are asked about their *happiness* or *satisfaction with life* (or a particular domain of it, such as work). Here, answers about happiness are taken to be affective responses, relating to feelings, and answers about satisfaction to be cognitively derived judgments. The responses along these two lines may be correlated but are distinct. Answers to questions that directly ask about happiness or satisfaction are generally less reliable than answers to longer survey instruments that ask about components of these states, and so the longer instruments are used in the best studies. Single questions are more likely to receive a facile, convenient, or expected answer. Examples of longer scales are the Oxford Happiness Inventory (Argyle *et al.* 1989) and the Satisfaction with Life Scale (Diener *et al.* 1985). Use of the more extensive questionnaires is especially called for when there is a cultural tendency to under- or over-state happiness or satisfaction. This sort of bias is more easily transmitted in responses to single questions.

Survey results along these lines have been found valid in a number of ways. By seeing if answers to questions correlate with a variety of measures that might reasonably be thought related to them – facial expressions reliably connected to emotional states, in-depth interviews by professionals and peers, persistence of answers over time, or answers to questions on components of either state – researchers have concluded that respondents do not seem to over- or understate their true situations. Argyle (2001: 15–18) summarizes a number of investigations of the adequacy of happiness and satisfaction measures. These measures on the whole possess a number of desirable properties: the items that make up the test tend to have high correlations with one another even though they are not rephrasings of the same question; they tend to give similar scores over time; they have reasonable validity characteristics (confirmations by friends, family, professionals, and so on) as already mentioned; and they seem not be subject to biases in reporting within countries, or these biases can be controlled. This is true of cross-sectional studies within a country or culture, but is less certain cross-culturally, where extra care needs to be taken in comparing results. Countries seem to differ in how acceptable it is to express positive or negative assessments, and whether social or group aspects of well-being are considered when reporting individual well-being.

Since happiness and satisfaction are aspects of well-being, and given the method of asking respondents to judge these states, these studies explore *subjective well-being* (Diener 1984; Diener *et al.* 1999). The contrasting method of trying to judge welfare empirically through measures such as income levels, educational attainment, health outcomes, and so on, is an *objective* approach.

Given the concentration in economics on statistics derived from objective data, and our choice to consider subjective data, we should explore the interesting relation between subjective and objective accounts of well-being. One feature of objective accounts is that they are partial: they miss what might be most important to well-being. Lane reports E. P. Thompson's response to the increasingly clear evidence that workers lived longer and ate better during the advent of the industrial revolution in England during the period from 1760 to 1815. "It is neither poverty nor disease but work itself which casts the blackest shadow over the years of the Industrial Revolution" (Thompson 1963: 211). Misery from routinized and excessive work was not reflected in the longevity and consumption statistics. It is difficult to see how objective data alone could be used to locate this failure of well-being.

Building on this distinction, authors have contrasted the *standard of living*, which concerns the material and other resources available for carrying on life, and the *quality of life* itself, whose measurement is less tangible, given that it has to do with the self and its relation to others (Nussbaum and Sen 1993; Lane 1991: 440–441). The standard of living may be assessed objectively, but the quality of life is essentially subjective. Allardt (1978) studied the relation between objective living standard measures and subjective life quality reports. On the whole, he found that the correlation between objective and subjective measures was zero or nearly zero. For example, income and satisfaction with work experience did not predict one another. The exception was a weak relation between the level of income and satisfaction with income. While Allardt's study is suggestive in pointing out that subjective and objective data are not obviously related, it was based on four Scandinavian countries and so may be limited in its applicability. More recent work suggests the following elaboration of Allardt's findings.

Diener and Suh (1997) reconsidered the relation of objective and subjective indicators of well-being in a much larger sample of forty countries. They found a correlation of 0.57 between subjective well-being and a quality of life index; this is of course much higher than Allardt's findings, and the case of the Scandinavian countries was re-confirmed in the new study. There are two problems with concluding that this implies a strong relationship, however. First, there were some notable discrepancies between the two measures. Argyle (2001: 19) points out that pairs of countries (Austria and Nigeria, for example) rate equally on subjective scales but one of them (Austria) is much higher on objective measures. Thus, despite the positive correlation, the relationship is not particularly tight. The more serious problem is the one mentioned earlier about differences in cultural norms in answering questions in this area. By the use of longer questionnaires the researchers have avoided some of this problem, but part of it probably remains and influences the results. On the whole, we can say that subjective and objective indicators of well-being are positively though not very strongly related to one another.

## The place of the economic in life satisfaction

Looking at studies of subjective well-being by themselves, we find some striking patterns relevant to the place of economic concerns in overall satisfaction. Lane concludes that "all the studies of subjective well-being [show] that it is satisfaction with family life and feelings of self-confidence and self-esteem that contribute most – far more than income – to a sense of well-being or to happiness, however measured" (Lane 1991: 443). Specifically on income, there is a modest relation between *satisfaction with* income (which is, of course, subjective) and a sense of well-being and a much smaller relation between well-being and income itself. Whether or not people are content with their incomes is more important to gauging their well-being than is knowledge of the levels of their incomes. We explore this matter in detail below.

Among the best predictors of life satisfaction are attitudes towards self including a sense of personal control, accomplishment, and an ability to deal with problems. A sense of internal control – the belief that one can influence what happens – is highly correlated with life satisfaction (Argyle 2001: 50–51). These are followed by satisfaction with relations with family, spouses, children, and friends (including number of friends). In most studies, attitudes towards work are also very good predictors of overall satisfaction. Evaluations of health, religious activities, and attitudes towards government make less of a contribution. It is possible for people to be very satisfied in these domains without achieving high levels of *overall* satisfaction. Finally, there does not seem to be the kind of hierarchy Maslow had in mind in the relation among satisfactions. In particular, Maslow suggests that only those who satisfy the lower four levels of needs and then reach the level of self-actualizing personal experiences can be happy.[2] This does not hold up to evidence. Needs are satisfied in a variety of orders. It even seems that satisfaction in different areas of life can be added to yield overall satisfaction (Campbell, Converse, and Rodgers 1981: 79).

Thus, the areas that relate to satisfaction best are largely personal and interpersonal. Except for the world of work, economic matters seem secondary. The economic matters that most closely relate to satisfaction are those that result in feelings of achievement and accomplishment deriving from work. Yet, given the importance often accorded to income (and consumption), we consider the role of income in detail.

### Income and life satisfaction

Studies of subjective well-being throw light on the relation of income to happiness and satisfaction. A central result is that more developed nations seem to have somewhat higher levels of happiness.

Overall, the more prosperous nationalities tend to be more satisfied, but the correlation is not very strong . . . Income and happiness are correlated at the national level, but the linkage is surprisingly weak. (Inglehart and Rabier 1986).

---

[2] The first four needs are physiological needs: safety, belongingness and love, and esteem. Further discussion of Maslow's model is in Chapter 3.

This picture can be modified in certain ways. To the extent that countries have different mixes of occupations and social ranks, and these have different levels of satisfaction associated with them, national comparisons may be misleading. When comparisons are made within such categories, the correlation between economic development and well-being rises to 0.60. Indeed, the same magnitude of correlation is seen in national studies that are more recent than Inglehart and Rabier's. Thus we might conclude that, cross-nationally, well-being and economic development are positively related.

However, the size of this effect is not large. That is, the difference between the average satisfactions in the richest and the poorest countries amounts to 7 out of 30 units on Diener's satisfaction with life scale (a quarter of the scale) (Argyle 2001: 137). This is a notable difference, but it is dwarfed by the disparity in income between the richest and poorest countries: the dispersion in income is far greater than the dispersion in life satisfaction.

Nevertheless, in a number of recent studies, covering as many as 28 countries, the correlation averaged over countries is in a tight range from 0.59 to 0.62 (Argyle 2001: 43). As is discussed next, this effect is not seen cross-sectionally within countries. Because of this, the explanation for this relation seems to lie at the level of countries rather than with individuals within countries. One hypothesis is that much of the correlation between income and life satisfaction across countries has to do with basic needs. As is argued in Chapter 4, the concept of basic needs and related concepts such as the needs hierarchy are not clear so there is reason to doubt the validity of investigations employing them. Yet Diener, Diener, and Diener (1995) tried to control for basic needs consumption in nations and still found that the correlation between these adjusted incomes and satisfaction to be between 0.35 and 0.37 on average. So a large part of this correlation remains unexplained even if we try to operationalize the concept of basic needs and make adjustments on its basis.

A second explanation seems more compelling. As nations become wealthier, they provide public or quasi-public goods such as education, health care, safety, parks and leisure facilities, participatory political systems, transportation, environmental amenities, and the like, that together are more closely related to life satisfaction than is income of individuals or the private goods it buys. Researchers have also found that aspects of modernity such as individualism and satisfaction with self-esteem and with freedom are stronger correlates of satisfaction in richer nations (Argyle 2001: 142, 185). What is striking is that the wealth of nations seems to be more important to the satisfaction of individuals than does the wealth of individuals; but the national wealth needs to be spent in ways that enhance individual satisfaction. Argyle (2001: 142) summarizes this interpretation of the data by saying that "there are other causes of happiness that are more important than money."

The correlation of well-being and the average income of nations may lead one to expect that income and well-being *within* countries will also be correlated. But this does not generally seem to be true. "Knowing people's incomes does not tell us a great deal about their general satisfaction with life" (Campbell 1981: 58). Correlations between income or socioeconomic status and well-being within countries, when they exist, are quite small. Even people with the lowest incomes seem to be fairly happy, though less so than others (Lane 1991: 526). In a recent study covering nineteen nations, Diener and Oishi (2002) report that the within-country correlation between income and life satisfaction is 0.13, which is very low. This result seems quite robust. The effects are somewhat larger at low levels of income and for poorer countries, but these are likely due to the effects of other variables such as education, skill development, and availability and quality of work, that are more tightly correlated with income at lower income levels and have a greater effect on life satisfaction. In other words, factors that prevent life from going well are intercorrelated with income at low levels and in poor countries; they cause the simple correlation between income and life satisfaction to be higher than its sole contribution would suggest.

Something similar happens with the relation between income and satisfaction. The effect of income on job satisfaction becomes zero once other factors are taken into account in a multiple regression setting (Clark and Oswald 1996). Moreover, as Argyle points out, the difference in satisfaction between the lowest and highest income groups is on average only 11 percent of the satisfaction scale range within countries (Diener and Oishi 2002).

There is another reason we might doubt that there is a large effect of income on well-being: changes in satisfaction during periods of income growth for individual countries. The notable feature here is lack of any trend. "There has been virtually no increase in subjective well-being during a period of greatly increased prosperity for many countries" (Argyle 2001: 131). Thus the United States, Western European countries, and Japan have seen income go up by factors of two, four, or six with no change in satisfaction. The correlation between *changes* in income and life satisfaction is virtually zero in these countries. The same relation for poorer countries, such as India and Mexico, is still very low, being under 0.10 (Argyle 2001: 138).

## Satisfaction with Income and Behavior

Despite the lack of a statistically demonstrable connection between income and life satisfaction, people *behave* as if they do not realize the absence of a lasting effect of income on satisfaction. In one study, Campbell *et al.* (1976) found that money was rated eleventh out of twelve domains in importance to its contribution to life satisfaction. Nevertheless, when respondents were asked specifically about whether they wanted more money or would act to acquire more, matters are different. Thus, according to one estimate, people in the United States tend to want income that is a quarter higher than their current level, irrespective of how much money they have (Lebergott 1968: 98). In general, people believe (erroneously) that increases in income will lead to happiness. The simple correlation between income and satisfaction with it within a sample of nineteen countries is on average 0.25 (Diener and Oishi 2002), which is not very strong. This means that satisfaction with income is positively correlated with income but weakly so. As just reported, once other factors are taken into account in a multiple regression setting, income and satisfaction with it are unrelated (Clark and Oswald 1996). This is striking: there is no relation between the level of income and how satisfied people are with it, yet people want more income.

What are we to make of these patterns? First, it seems that people adapt quickly to whatever income level they attain. Thus short-lived increases in happiness result from increased income (and sharper decreases result from income losses), but happiness seems to return quickly to a baseline level. This accounts both for people wanting more income regardless of how much they have, and for the weak relation between income and satisfaction.[3]

There is another reason for the weak relation between income and well-being. The main sources of satisfaction lie outside the realm of income. Juster and Courant (1986: 165–166), in their time-use studies, report that the things that matter most for satisfaction, such as family, friendships, and work, are largely unaffected by differences in income. Juster (1985) identifies the main rewards of economic activity as involving making and doing – rather than having – and these are closely connected to work (and also to leisure). Andrews and Withey (1976) report that a sense of being effective in the world is what relates best to

---

[3] People do seem to care quite a bit, however, if they feel they are paid unfairly – that is, less than others in a similar situation. This seems to be the biggest predictor of dissatisfaction with pay (Berkowitz *et al.* 1987). This is important in our discussion below of satisfaction with work.

satisfaction. What income provides does not have the same impact on satisfaction or happiness. As is discussed below, job satisfaction is not evaluated primarily in terms of pay.

For all of these reasons, income and life satisfaction are not closely related. Yet we also know that people want more income and believe it will lead to greater well-being. Campbell summarizes the paradox:

> It has repeatedly been shown that when people are asked how the quality of their lives might be improved, they tend to answer in terms of more money . . . People appear to overestimate the beneficial effects that additional income will have on their lives . . . but its ability to enhance these feelings appears to be restricted to those material domains of life which relate to the need for having, which in turn has only a limited relationship to a person's general sense of well-being. (Campbell 1981: 66)

Thus the paradox is that even while people can accurately report *whether* they are happy or satisfied, they cannot accurately state *what* will make them happy. Indeed, in the main studies of subjective well-being, there was a slight *negative* correlation between what people said was important to satisfaction in their lives and what the data showed was important (Andrews and Withey 1976: 242–243; and Campbell, Converse, and Rodgers 1976: 82–93). "People are not clear about what really makes them happy or what the consequences are of various patterns that are central to their lives" (Wachtel 1983: 288). In related findings based on survey work, happiness is lower for those who judge their success by the amount of possessions even when they succeed in acquiring them (Dittmar 1992), or for those who rate financial success highly (Chan and Joseph 2000). Thus a common orientation towards consumption and financial success seems self-defeating.

This suggests that there are two kinds of rationality that are important to people. The one that neoclassical economists have concentrated on is finding the procedure to effect given goals. But it turns out that the goals that many people have are not those that lead to the best outcomes for them. So a second type of rationality goes beyond finding an effective procedure and focuses on determining the goals that align best with overall satisfaction. "Thus a man could be judged irrational either because his preferences are contradictory or because his desires and aversions do not reflect his pleasures and pains" (Tversky and Kahneman 1981: 458). The second type of irrationality is closely related to inauthenticity or self-alienation (Lane 1991: 550–553).

We now have seen considerable evidence on what makes lives go well. This evidence does not support an exclusive focus on income as the source of well-being. Economic influences on life satisfaction rank lower

than personal and interpersonal matters broadly construed. In the economic realm, work has the closest relation to satisfaction with life. In one
way, this is not surprising. We spend much more time at work than in
any other economically related activity. What happens at work should
affect our well-being simply for this reason. But work also relates much
more closely to personal fulfillment, which is a key to life satisfaction.
Given the salience of work to life satisfaction, let us consider it more
closely.

### Aspects of work

Given the doubts we might have about work being done simply for pay,
we question the identification of work with disutility. In looking at the
satisfaction that derives from work, we can consider some aspects of
human development that are closely related to work and life satisfaction
(Lane 1991). One of these has to do with cognitive complexity. We will
see that cognitive complexity is required and enhanced by job complexity. It involves the use of concepts that are held flexibly so that they
can be revised in the face of evidence and argument. Alongside this
conceptual sophistication is a capacity for abstraction, analysis, and
synthesis. Involved also is an ability to think counterfactually and to plan
ahead. One can see how these abilities would be associated with
rewarding work but that they would not be called upon for simple,
repetitive, and boring tasks. Thus, regarding this quality, "it is not
affluence but what people do for a living that determines their cognitive
development" (Lane 1991: 135).

Another connection between work and satisfaction emerges when
work provides a sense of personal effectiveness, so that the worker feels
responsible for shaping his or her life and feels an ability to affect the
world. Finally, we might consider self-esteem. Lane reports that this
feeling is unrelated to income (after a small minimum has been reached)
but is related to challenge and discretion on the job. Self-esteem does
not derive from equality of incomes, as some have suggested. Evidence
indicates that self-esteem is only modestly related to perceptions of
income inequality (Lane 1991: 200–201). Lane writes that:

the route to higher and more equal self-esteem is not so much through equaliza-
tion of incomes as through policies that improve the condition of the poor,
increase education, and especially promote work redesign that makes work more
challenging and rewarding. (Lane 1991: 200)

The connection between the economy and self-esteem seems to operate via work and skills rather than through the distribution of income. If

self-esteem, personal effectiveness, and cognitive development are desirable – and they are often mentioned as attributes that the poor lack – it is important to understand that these qualities are all the more likely to be developed through work rather than by an infusion of income.

### Effects of work

In the neoclassical framework, labor is treated as an input and goods and services as outputs. What this means is that the *processes* of work are ignored for their effects on welfare. As Scitovsky (1977: 133) put it, in the neoclassical framework "exchange is the source and proof of all economic gain, which explains the economist's preoccupation with it." Thus, in general, the bulk of writing in neoclassical economics is silent on the effects of work on the worker. Alfred Marshall, who referred to classical themes in his writings, was an exception. He held that:

the business by which a person earns his livelihood fills his thoughts during by far the greatest part of those hours in which his mind is at its best: during them his character is being formed by the ways in which he uses his faculties at work. (Marshall 1895: 1)

Marshall was echoing classical writings. Several classical economists discussed the effects of work on the worker. Thus Adam Smith asserted that work has long-lasting impacts on workers' personalities. Smith felt that the "understandings of the greater part of men are necessarily formed by their ordinary employments." Repetitive, boring yet demanding jobs, cause a worker to "become as stupid and ignorant as it is possible for a human creature to become" (Smith 1937: 734–735). Marx suggested, in his discussion of alienated labor, that fulfilling labor was not possible under capitalism, which inevitably had a corrosive effect on workers (Chapter 2).

There are, then, two questions to consider. First, with the progress of capitalist development, are there decreasing opportunities for work that will be beneficial for workers beyond the pay that employment provides? To answer this, we need to consider the literature on deskilling inspired by Marx. Second, in modern capitalist economies, what evidence do we have on the effect of work on workers' personalities? We can answer this by looking at empirical studies of work and personality change. Reflecting on the literature on deskilling helps us answer the following questions. Has work over time become degraded so that it is no longer satisfying? In particular, has the process of industrialization acted to make humans more like machines? Is there a fundamental tendency in industrial or capitalist economies toward reducing the skill content of work, such that workers can no longer have fulfilling jobs? These issues are relevant for many reasons. For example, if work has been degraded as feared, it is more and more likely that the only reason to work is to gain money and thereby endure disutility.

In surveying the relevant empirical literature, we find that on the whole there has not been a tendency in the twentieth century for US workers to become more machine-like while working, even if many of them are working more and more with machines. Partly this is true since the changing mix of work has favored growth of service-sector jobs at the expense of manufacturing and agricultural jobs, which are more susceptible to automation. To the extent that machines have replaced unskilled work, this tendency is also held back. Finally, many machines require greater skills to design, operate, and repair; thus an upgrading rather than downgrading of skills has often been required of workers. We will consider the matter in more detail but, all in all, the evidence is that adoption of machinery has not led to boredom, loss of satisfaction, and reduced learning on the job for men and women. In fact, for men, introduction of machines has had the opposite tendency (Lane 1991: 272–223; 276–277).

Lane presents evidence that workers "develop cognitive complexity, self-esteem and social responsibility at work primarily if their jobs are substantively complex, that is, if their jobs require complex skills" (1991: 283).[4] Thus, from the point of view of seeing whether there are adequate opportunities for work that is rewarding, we must determine if deskilling has occurred. *Deskilling* refers to the tendency, often argued to be manifested under capitalist development, for workers' skills to be simplified and degraded as much as possible. Braverman (1974) and Edwards (1979) have argued that deskilling is a process that is likely to take place as a result of capitalist development, relating it to tendencies they discern in the twentieth-century workplace. Braverman sees the capitalist devising machines and routinizing work activities so as to seize control over work from the workers themselves. This process of deskilling takes from workers knowledge that once was specific only to them. Marx cited W. Thompson who wrote that "'Knowledge' becomes 'an instrument,' capable of being detached from labour and opposed to it" (Marx 1977a: 483). With this knowledge of the production process, the capitalist can design machines that replace or routinize previously complex and satisfying work. Edwards adds that for the most part the motive for deskilling is to reduce costs. By deskilling work, capitalists are able to hire the cheapest workers. But, whatever the precise motive for it,

---

[4] The remainder of this section relies on Lane (1991: 283–288).

both authors argue that deskilling is a manifest tendency of capitalist development.

We might then consider whether on the whole deskilling has occurred. Sabel (1982) suggests that, when deskilling results from the introduction of machines, it matters who services and maintains the machines. If formerly highly skilled workers do, then some deskilling likely takes place. Yet if enough unskilled workers end up doing this, a net increase in skilled work occurs. Korunka *et al.* (1995) take a similar approach and confirm that the effect of new technology differs according to who ends up with less skilled, and who with more skilled, jobs. Investigations along these lines have been inconclusive as to the overall effect of technical change, however (Lane 1991: 286–287).

Another approach is to categorize jobs by skill content and to see how the mix of jobs has changed over time (Lane 1991). Form (1981) finds that in the United States there was some deskilling in the thirty years before 1900, but that since then trends have changed. In the subsequent seventy years, he found little change in skilled work performed by women. For women, service work increased as domestic work declined, and the proportion of other job categories remained roughly constant. For men, on the other hand, skilled jobs increased overall, as there was a slow rise in skilled jobs and a rapid decline in unskilled jobs. He concludes that the amount of skilled work has not decreased over the past seventy years and has probably increased. If this is so, the only way for Braverman's or Edwards' argument to hold would be to assume that the skill content of today's skilled jobs is lower than it had been for the older skilled jobs. Spenner (1979) considered this issue further, examining manufacturing and service jobs. Some jobs were of course downgraded, but a larger number required greater skills and freedom from close supervision. Following up on this research, he found little change in workers' control over work content, work initiative, and the manner and speed of work (Spenner 1983). From this US evidence, we can conclude that there has historically been some deskilling of work but that, more recently, the skill content of work has either remained constant or has improved (Lane 1991). Indeed, one recent study looking at the United Kingdom presents evidence that there has been a significant increase in the skills used from the introduction of advanced technology (Gallie *et al.* 1998). The opportunities to exercise skills in work have not disappeared.

While the evidence referred to earlier suggests that the skill content of US jobs has not declined, it is also true that there are routinized jobs. People who work in them might well say that they are working primarily for pay. Workers in these jobs are likely to see the alternative as unemployment rather than a better job. These workers would prefer a more rewarding job if one were offered; it is just that this choice is not available. Following from this, we would expect higher unemployment to mean that those holding routinized jobs would feel increasingly fortunate (to have a job at all). Indeed, in surveys, those who hold routinized jobs express increased satisfaction with them as unemployment within their ranks rose, in contrast to the opposite pattern seen for those in more rewarding jobs (Lane 1991: 391). Working primarily for pay "is quickly abandoned if intrinsic returns become more available: intrinsic rewards undermine the importance of extrinsic rewards" (Greenberg 1980: 269). Lane (1991: 402) also reports evidence that in jobs where creativity is required, intrinsic motivation – that deriving from the work itself – is "usually necessary," pay being insufficient.

Routine tasks require only the learning of a fixed procedure. How to succeed at the job merely requires the worker to implement this procedure. There is nothing absorbing in the work itself. In creative tasks, success involves solving problems that cannot be solved simply by recourse to formulas and procedures.

### Pay and personality

We can now turn to the issue of what benefits workers derive from jobs and what they value in them. Do workers see work's benefit deriving mainly from pay or do they see it deriving from other work characteristics? We also need to know whether work in a capitalist economy such as the United States has become so routinized and boring that the effect on personalities is mainly deadening.

As the work of Jencks, Perlman, and Rainwater (1988: 1328, 1343) suggests (Lane 1991: 342), it is job characteristics rather than pay that seem to be the primary features of what makes for good jobs. They conclude that "the combined effect of nonmonetary job characteristics on job ratings is more than twice that of earnings. Equating a job's overall desirability with pay is therefore quite likely to be misleading." The matter is complicated by workers' imperfect knowledge of jobs they do not actually perform. Prior to taking jobs, workers are likely to rate jobs on the basis of easily discernible features such as pay and occupational title. "As a result, they probably put more weight on pay when making prospective judgments than when making retrospective ones."

A study by Juster and Courant (1986) provides more insight into work satisfaction. They had people keep logs of their activities in which they noted the level of satisfaction registered while doing them. Among the aspects of work that determined satisfaction were challenge and learning on the job, whether work required initiative and creativity or whether is was boring or repetitious, whether the work entailed significant responsibility (especially true for men), and whether co-workers provided good company. Pay was mentioned less often than these intrinsic attributes (Juster and Courant 1986: 155–158).[5] Similarly, Argyle (2001: 109) writes that "Job satisfaction is increased by pay though not much, and more by work that has features such as the use of skills, autonomy and skill variety." The correlation between pay and job satisfaction is usually between 0.15 and 0.17 (Argyle 2001: 91). Rather than being a secondary feature, as implied by the compensating differentials model, job characteristics are the primary determinant of job quality.

The main study of the effects of work on workers' personalities is by Kohn and Schooler (1983), which Lane summarizes (1991: 242). First, they characterize good jobs. These are jobs that have "substantive complexity," which they argue "stands as the keystone of the entire jobs structure – affected by and affecting many other job conditions," finding it to be "at the core of highly placed, responsible, demanding but rewarding jobs" (Kohn and Schooler 1983: 136). Job complexity means challenging activity performed in an atmosphere without close supervision, thus allowing for creativity, discretion, and judgment by the worker. On the other hand, doing work with little cognitive complexity leads to feelings of alienation (Kohn and Schooler 1983: 18). Second, complex jobs attract workers who themselves display cognitive complexity, which we discussed earlier, but they also reinforce and develop this quality in workers. Thus the relation between worker attributes and job attributes is reciprocal and reinforcing (Kohn and Schooler 1983: 77, 118). The third conclusion relates to self-direction. Self-directedness is also reciprocally determined: it attracts those possessing this quality and enhances it in them. It is also associated with many positive psychological traits (Kohn and Schooler 1983: 142, 148, 150). Finally, the effects of job type carry over into leisure activities. Thus, an intellectually challenging job is associated with intellectually demanding leisure activities (Lane 1991: 248–249). Complementing the effect of work on leisure is the effect of education, which influences not only leisure but also the quality of work a person may do (Argyle 2001: 45).

As we might suspect from previously reported findings, education primarily affects well-being not through income but through occupational

---

[5] In the psychology literature, intrinsically motivated behavior is defined as behavior engaged in by a person so as to feel competent and self-determining (Deci 1975: 61). Work can be such an activity.

choice (Witter, Okun, Stock, and Haring 1984). Similarly, the main effects of education on quality of life are through satisfying work, increased control over aspects of one's life, and better access to social support (Ross and Van Willigen 1997). The centrality of work is underlined by the finding that work satisfaction is more important to non-work satisfaction than the other way around:

job satisfaction has a greater influence on life or nonwork satisfaction than vice versa . . . work attitudes and experiences are major determinants of nonwork behaviors and attitudes. (Chacko 1983: 163)

This last point gains salience because leisure activities are broadly important to life satisfaction (Argyle and Martin 1991: 90–92). Thus work can influence life satisfaction in two ways: through its own effects and, indirectly, through the effects it has on leisure.

Kohn and Schooler find survey evidence to support the view that people's work has significant effects on them: it can increase the very qualities that are required for desirable work, and it can influence leisure time activities. Another piece of evidence for the psychological benefits of work derives from studies of paid work done by married women. Since their husbands did not take up a corresponding share of work around the home, these women worked longer hours than married women without paid work, yet their mental health was no worse, and they indeed showed fewer signs of stress and distress (Hall 1986: 4, cited in Lane 1991: 258).

It can be difficult for those wedded to the neoclassical framework to accept that work could be valuable in itself. We have already mentioned the reason for this: the idea is at variance with the economist's model of the amount of work supplied resulting from the disutility incurred to satisfy a demand for goods and services. This sort of thinking, particularly the view that work is motivated only by the prospect of compensation predates neoclassical economics and is typified by Bentham's strong statement:

Desire for labour for the sake of labour – of labour considered in the character of an end, without any view to anything else, is a sort of desire that seems scarcely to have place in the human breast.
                    (Bentham 1954: 427, cited in Lane 1991: 370)

Scitovsky understood the importance of work to the satisfaction of workers and held that differences in work satisfaction could well outweigh differences based on income (1977: 104). It is well known that satisfactions associated with work would not be included in standard measures of economic welfare. Thus:

Work can be pleasant or unpleasant . . . Those effects of work are completely missing from the economists's numerical index of economic welfare [which is] *not* net of the disutility of labor that went into producing it, nor does it include the satisfaction of labor . . . [which] is not an economic good because it does not go through the market and its value is not measurable. (Scitovsky 1977: 90)

In fact, if undesirable work is better compensated than desirable work, an economy with more undesirable work will have a higher national product. The pleasure or displeasure that occurs during an activity is distinct from that deriving from the outcome. The benefits arising from such activities can be labeled "instrumental outputs" (to be distinguished from ultimate outputs) or "process goods" (Juster and Stafford 1985: 3–4). So, for example, the products of work are different from the activity of work itself. The activity itself can be found to be valuable, which would be a good thing since work takes up a very large portion of people's time.

Even if pay does not have the paramount role that neoclassical theory would assign it, it does have a role. One way to think about how job characteristics and pay are perceived has been put forward by Herzberg and his associates (Herzberg, Mausner, and Snyderman 1959). On the basis of the evidence they collect, these authors argue that the *satisfactions* associated with work are primarily intrinsic and have to do with the characteristics of the job as they relate to the worker's goals and desires. If these are not present, the worker is not *dis*satisfied, but is merely indifferent. Job *dissatisfactions* are primarily extrinsic and include pay, the nature of supervision and the like. These can all be fine, yet a worker will be merely indifferent unless the intrinsic satisfactions of the job are present. This theory explains why a well-paying job can be unsatisfying: it can be so if it is boring, repetitive, allows for little creativity, and so forth. The framework also explains the finding, reported earlier, that workers can become quite upset if they feel that they are unfairly paid, since pay can be a source of dissatisfaction. The theory is also in accord with the finding that feelings of competence are better predictors of life satisfaction than is income (Campbell 1981: ch. 13). Consequently, it fits well with the evidence we presented that shows a weak relation between income and well-being.

We can put what we have said so far about work and satisfaction in the language of skill. In research reported by Argyle (2001: 92–93), workers were asked if they would choose the same jobs again if they had a choice. The importance of the use of skills in the jobs that would be chosen again is striking. Occupations at the top of the list, those with nine-tenths or four-fifths of current holders saying they would repeat the job, are jobs for mathematicians, lawyers, and journalists; somewhat lower are skilled printers, car workers, and steel workers. At the bottom of the list are unskilled car workers and steel workers, with only one-sixth or one-fifth saying they would do the same job again. In general, it seems that skills as well as autonomy in work along with appropriate feedback make for satisfying work. "Two hundred studies have found that job satisfaction does correlate with these job characteristics" (Argyle 2001: 92).[6]

Interestingly, job satisfaction increases with age, but it does not seem to have much relation to gender. "Many American studies have found no difference in job satisfaction between men and women. However, a large-scale British study found that women were more satisfied than men" (Argyle 2001: 95). Losing a job does have striking effects on physical and mental health and on well-being generally. This not surprising, but the magnitude of this effect is notable. Argyle (2001: 103) considers "unemployment and the fear of losing jobs [to be] one of the greatest sources of unhappiness in the modern world."

> Unemployment is a major source of unhappiness in the modern world. It produces depression, suicide, ill health, apathy, low self-esteem – every aspect of low satisfaction and unhappiness. The effect is quite strong ... is causal ... [and] holds up when other variables have been controlled, such as income. (Argyle 2001: 44)

Not only have authors argued for the influence of work on personality but some have also suggested that work and identity are closely related. Thus Eric Erikson considered that too close a link between work and identity leaves the latter incomplete and can be harmful, yet he suggested that work is crucial to identity. Along with "an intelligible theory of the processes of life," work that arises from a "'conflict free' habitual use of a dominant faculty to be elaborated in an *occupation*" is crucial to identity formation (Erikson 1956, cited in Lane 1991: 254). Identities are "more fruitful and reliable" when they are attained with some effort rather than acquired passively (Bourne 1978). This suggests that achievement is more important than group-derived feelings of worth. Indeed, self-esteem and happiness are more closely related to *achievement* than to aspects of personhood such as citizenship or membership in a particular group or community (Lane 1991: 187).

Many writers argue that political participation contributes importantly to life satisfaction.[7] However, the evidence suggests that the causality between feelings of confidence or self-esteem on the one hand, and membership in political organizations, political participation or leadership on the other, is the opposite of what these writers might

---

[6] Work satisfaction is also clearly related to life satisfaction. A meta-analysis of many studies puts the correlation at 0.44 (reported by Argyle 2001: 90).
[7] Even if it does not, there may be other reasons, of course, for pursuing it.

anticipate. Those who take part in such activities already have self-esteem and confidence. Those who do not seem to be outside social networks that deal with distant-seeming public issues, while matters of personal effectiveness for the individuals concerned are more pressing and are not adequately resolved (Lane 1991: 187). Self-esteem seems to be a more private matter than political participation.

We now have a number of conclusions that affect how we might think about poverty. Despite what individuals may perceive, the sources of increased subjective well-being do not lie in increased income or consumption. In fact, such matters are not in the first rank of issues that affect well-being, which depends more on personal feelings of self-worth and interpersonal relations with intimates, friends, and family. Among economic concerns, complex and engaging work, requiring creativity and use of skills, is the best predictor of life satisfaction. Workers value these characteristics of jobs much more than the pay they provide. Rather than something to be avoided, creative, skilled work is a significant contributor to life satisfaction. Contrary to what many might expect, income is poorly related to happiness or life satisfaction. The relation between income and satisfaction among countries, and at low income levels, is best explained by the lack of publicly provided facilities for education, health, safety, political participation, and the like, which may be correlated with income but are distinct from it.

The remedy for poverty, then, is not to provide income or "make-work" jobs that have little to recommend them besides their remuneration. If we are to increase welfare, these are not the main avenues to pursue. The most important economic factor in poverty, interpreted as a failure of well-being, is the lack of meaningful work or of the capacity to do it when it is available.

# 9    The psychology of work

## Introduction

In this chapter, we explore the meaning work has for the individual. This meaning is expressed in the individual's emotional investment in work. Our emotions mark the significance objects, activities, and persons have for us. The importance of emotions lies in the way they provide the individual with "an orientation toward the world," a "framework through which the world is viewed" (Lear 1990: 51–52). This orientation is not, however, of the sort provided by a map or a compass. The difference lies both in the nature of the space we find ourselves in, and in the nature of the orientation we need within it. The space in which our emotions orient us, unlike the physical space of the map or compass, is the interpersonal space of relatedness with others. Furthermore, maps and compasses offer a sense of position in space, whereas emotions invest our position in space with its significance. Our emotions tell us what matters and what does not; and they tell us how it matters, especially whether it is good for us or poses a danger to our well-being. The emotional orientation is subject to distortion and the guidance it provides is not always accurate. It is, nonetheless, vital to any study that concerns itself with the meaningful orientation of the individual in the space of interaction and social organization. To understand the significance of work, we need then to consider its emotional meaning, or the emotional connection the individual has to it, which is the subject we will refer to here as the psychology of work. We will consider this psychology of work from a specific angle, which is the connection of work to human desires and to the formative relationships through which we seek and sometimes achieve the satisfaction of desire.[1]

Our orientation in a world of self and other has an enduring quality. While emotions can be momentary and pass by with little residue, they can also establish enduring qualities of objects in emotional space. In

---

[1] A more appropriate term for desire's object would be gratification, but satisfaction is the more commonly used term in political economy, and we will follow that usage here.

doing so, they establish what we might refer to as emotional configurations: systems in which objects, especially human objects (others), take on an enduring meaning rooted in a more or less permanent attributed relationship with the satisfaction of desire, and the fear that desire will not be satisfied.

We will take it as a premise that the emotional configurations shaping the meaning of work are formed early in life, and, though they may evolve to express or play out primitive issues and conflicts, their underlying meaning does not undergo any radical transformation in most cases. The enduring quality of emotional investments follows from the fact that to change the configuration of emotional meaning is to change the organization of the individual's inner psychic or emotional life. If our premise regarding the enduring quality of emotional configuration is correct, it follows that, to understand the psychology of work, we must first understand something of what happens in early emotional development that bears on the individual's relationship with work.

In some ways, the work that has been done to explore and depict early emotional experience and early emotional development has a somewhat speculative quality. We have limited access to the emotional life of infants. The methods used to provide information concerning early cognitive development are not easily applied to the formative process of psychic structure, or what we refer to above as emotional configurations.[2] These configurations and the processes by which they emerge and develop have been studied through infant observation and through the admittedly impressionistic method of analyzing memories, dreams, and emotional experiences in adult life. Because of the nature of the data available, the image constructed of emotional development, a selected part of which is summarized below, should be considered less a scientifically grounded set of hypotheses than a form of intellectual speculation based on extensive information developed from the study of both adult and childhood experience.

In any case, our interest here is not in infant and childhood emotional development for its own sake, but for what light it might shed on the meaning of work in adult life. To understand that meaning, we have taken a developmental approach that treats the adult construction of work as a product of a long and difficult development, and which can best be understood as the result of that development and not as a freestanding construction. What this means is that the adult does not decide to invest a consciously and freely chosen meaning in work. Adults do not

---

[2] Important work has been done on infant and early childhood emotional development, most notably Spitz (1965), Mahler *et al.* (1975), and Stern (1985).

adopt and reject various meanings as suits their needs and interests at particular moments of time. Rather, the adult meaning is an expression of an irreversible development. It has a power over the individual more than the individual has power over it. Indeed, it is a part of the shaping of the person that then governs how that person experiences meaning, makes choices, and orients him or her self in an adult world.

Our interest is in this last process of shaping meaning and finding an orientation in an adult world. The brief excursus into early emotional development is meant to highlight the possible meanings of work that emerge as a product of that development, to see what that meaning really expresses about the individual and the society in which he or she works. The meaning we attribute to the infant is also the meaning the adult experiences, albeit in a new form suitable to adult mental life and adult forms of communication.

## Emotional development and the meaning of work

If the psychology of work begins with early emotional development, it begins with the parent–child relationship.[3] This relationship shapes the meaning work will take on for the individual, the psychological ends it is hoped work will achieve, and the obstacles and limits the individual discovers in his or her capacity to do work of different kinds. This is a complex subject. We limit ourselves to basic considerations relevant to the matter of the fit between character and work, and the psychological preconditions for developing the kinds of skills that can secure entry of the worker into civil society. First, we will summarize relevant aspects of the parent–child relationship.[4]

(1) The infant exists in a state of absolute dependence on its parent, normally its mother. This is not simply a matter of physical dependence for the means of physical survival, but also of psychological dependence for psychological survival, which is to say survival as a nascent person. The nascent person requires that attention be paid not only to bodily needs, but also to emotional needs, including the needs "to feel affirmed, confirmed, recognized . . . accepted and appreciated" (Wolf 1988: 55). These emotional needs can be summarized in the following way: the infant needs to feel emotionally or psychically alive, and, for it to feel alive in this sense, its original vitality must be nurtured in the relationship with its parent. To be psychically alive means to be the

---

[3] We use the term "parent" here to refer to the child's primary caretaker, who may or may not be the child's biological parent.

[4] This account is adapted from Winnicott (1960a).

origin or source of emotional experience, which we are when we can make an emotional investment in objects (in this case the parent) that is encouraged and accepted. This encouragement and acceptance is expressed in the mirroring for us of our emotional experience by our parent, who in sharing it with us assures that it can exist in the world of interaction with others, and in this sense is real.

The infant's absolute dependence on the parent means that the satisfaction of need takes place wholly within the parent–infant relationship. Because at the outset this dependence is so absolute, the infant begins its life not as a separate person related to others on which it depends, but as a part of a unit including the parent (Winnicott 1960: 39). This condition, which is not essentially a relationship, is not the means to survival, but a state of being.

(2) In the state of primitive dependence, the infant's needs are either met or they are not according to the rhythm of its relationship with its parent. The more adequate a job the parent does in meeting the infant's need, the less the infant will experience a distinction between need and satisfaction. The more need and satisfaction have the same meaning, the more the need is experienced to bring about satisfaction. Thus, the infant need do nothing to secure satisfaction beyond expressing its need, and often enough satisfaction arrives on schedule, so that expressing need is not even necessary. We can, nonetheless, distinguish three important modalities of this relationship, one in which need immediately creates satisfaction and the two are merged, one in which satisfaction is only brought into being after the overt expression of need, and one in which the infant's need must be adapted to that of the parent if it is to be satisfied.

In the first of these modalities, the source of satisfaction appears in anticipation of the infant's need for it. This suggests an emotional and physical connection between parent (often the mother) and infant of a particularly powerful and effective type, one within which the issue of separate realities for the two participants does not arise. Winnicott suggests that this relationship validates an illusion that the infant has the power to control the source of satisfaction, to make satisfaction happen simply by needing it. In this illusion the infant's desire is endowed with what, viewed from outside the illusion, we would describe as a magical power. However illusory this power may seem viewed from outside the relationship, it has nonetheless a certain reality within that relationship, at least for a period of time. According to Winnicott, by nurturing this illusion, the parent also nurtures the infant's nascent sense of itself as a creative force. That is, this primitive illusion is the starting point for what in adult life we would refer to as creativity and the capacity for creative living. As we suggest in the chapter on creativity, the creative stance toward the world incorporates something of the divine. By adopting it, we imagine ourselves sharing in a capability we might otherwise restrict to a divine power.

However close the connection between mother and infant, they do not exist wholly within the same world of experience. Rather they are, at least in nascent state, two separable centers of experience. This separation is felt, for example, when the mother does not anticipate the infant's need perhaps because of the intervention of her own. When this happens, the infant must assert its self, which is to say, assert its separate need and implicitly the existence of its self as a separate center of experience. The child does this for example by crying and other measures employed to gain its parent's attention and the satisfaction of its need that only she can provide. While this assertion may be intended to reestablish the primitive state in which mother and infant are merged, it also signals the limits of that state and the inevitability that another state, in which separation is the rule, will replace it.

This effort to gain the parent's attention for its need, which is to say for its self, suggests a second modality for the relation between need and satisfaction, one in which the infant must do something to secure satisfaction of its need. When this succeeds, the infant also succeeds in making the source of satisfaction respond to it, which is to say the infant succeeds in reasserting its self as the center of the shared experience it has with its parent. The infant may not however succeed in accomplishing this end, with the result that a struggle ensues over the locus of the center of emotional experience in the relationship, which is now shifting over to the parent.

When the center of emotional experience shifts away from the infant, it is in a sense lost to it. This happens especially when the infant comes to see in the assertion of its need, and therefore in need itself, a threat to its relationship with its parent. If the parent cannot adapt to the infant's need, but requires that the infant make the adaptation, for example by having its need when the parent wants to or is prepared to satisfy that need, the infant is put in a position of adaptation to the parent, who makes it clear that the assertion of the infant's own need cannot be tolerated. When experiences of this kind come to dominate the relationship, and, in Winnicott's language, the parent is not "good enough," the infant risks losing its sense of itself as a creative source and origin. The parent, for example, responds to the infant's assertion of its need with anger or withdrawal, signaling to the infant that if it wants to preserve the relation with the parent it must be on the basis of adaptation to or compliance with the parent's needs.

The result is that the infant loses the sense of itself as the origin of experience, as a creative center or a "center of initiative in the world" (Kohut 1977). Winnicott refers to this creative center and origin of experience as the "true self," and suggests that when the infant must adapt to the rhythm of its parent to have its need satisfied, it must repress its true self and construct an alternative, or "false self" based on the principle not of creativity, but of compliance (Winnicott 1960b; see also Bollas 1989). The repression of the true self in a relationship means the loss of the experience of psychic and emotional aliveness. This loss, which is also loss of the capacity for creative living, has a meaning on an emotional level comparable to that of death on the physical level.

(3) The infant's "inherited potential includes a tendency towards growth and development" (Winnicott 1960a: 43), which means a tendency to establish a separate existence as a unit on its own, a center of experience distinct from the parent. This development of a separate existence as a psychological entity in its own right brings with it the need to cope with both internal and external realities, especially intrapsychic reality and interpsychic (or interpersonal) reality. It also means that the infant's, now the child's, original vitality and capacity for creative living must take on a form appropriate for a world that it does not control, and cannot imagine itself controlling. The existence of a world outside, which is an alternative reality to the psychic reality of the inner world, establishes for the child the task of developing a creative orientation to a reality it does not control.

The parent either encourages and facilitates this development, or treats it as a threat. Again, the issue of whether the relation with the parent is a real relationship, one in which two separate, or at least incipiently separate, centers of experience relate or interact is vital. The possibility of creative living in adult life, including creativity in work, depends on the meaning separation takes on for parent and child. The struggle between creativity and compliance, so central to Winnicott's conception of early emotional development, will play itself out in the world of work in ways vital to understanding the meaning of poverty and the prospects for freedom in work.

Does work mean subordination to the will of others and thus a recreation of an early emotional experience requiring the suppression of a separate self-experience to preserve the relationship with the other? Or, does work mean the creative engagement between an autonomous center of experience and an external world? Put another way, does the way society organizes work require workers who have preserved and developed their capacity for creative living, or does it require that workers suppress that capacity, which they can do best when they have learned to do so early in life?

(4) In the child's development into a separate psychological unit, a residue of dependence remains, especially as a tendency to regress to a state reminiscent of the earlier state of absolute dependence and absence of differentiation. The relationship between this residue and the tendency toward growth and development helps shape the meaning work will take on for the individual. The residue of this primitive state of dependence fosters an impulse to avoid work and count on the expectation that need will be satisfied on demand, simply because we demand it, or by the intervention of a powerful, if not omnipotent, other, rather than by our work.

The more powerful this residue, the more the individual will see work in the context of a wish to recreate and secure the needed relationship that overcomes separation and secures dependence on a reliable caretaker, or that in some way expresses the psychological condition of dependence. Specifically, the individual will want to recreate the relationship between need and satisfaction that develops in the primitive relationship, whether the two are one or they are distinguished, whether need must be impressed on the parent if it is to be satisfied, or whether need must be adapted to the needs of the parent.

In sum, achieving the state of emotional separation means that the individual has developed the capacity to think and to act as a separate center of initiative and experience. Separation from the parent, which depends on the parent's capacity to recognize and respond to the infant and young child's separate need and experience, is a necessary condition for the development of autonomy, and therefore creativity. Freedom understood as the capacity for creative living depends on the capacity of the parent–child relationship to nurture and facilitate the child's separate emotional being.

The central meaning the parent–child relationship has for the child is satisfaction. The significance of work develops out of the way satisfaction is defined within this relationship. So far as need creates, or is perceived to create, satisfaction, no distinction between need and satisfaction develops, and the infant need do nothing to assure satisfaction. The issue of work does not arise. This situation cannot, however, persist indefinitely, nor can it be sustained continuously. Parental failure, even if it is no more than a failure in timing satisfaction according to the rhythm of the infant's need, promotes a rupture between need and satisfaction that can set the infant along the road leading to work. And, even without parental failure, the child's pursuit of a separate reality, which is to say a reality separate from that sustained within the circumference of the parent–infant bond, leads in the direction of work, even if a long period still remains before the infant will have the experience of real work.

## Work and satisfaction

Only when separation reaches the point where the parent cannot and will not provide what the child needs simply because he or she needs it, or when the child is not satisfied with what the parent has to offer, does the question of work arise. Now the child must look outside the relationship with the parent to find a way of gaining satisfaction. This finding satisfaction in the external world leads us in the direction of work, and gives work its psychological meaning. Up to this moment, the primary route to satisfaction is not work, but direct access to an imagined source of the good things that we want. This source is the creator, holder, and provider of what is good, which is the object of our desire. To acquire that object, or those objects, we must get them from their source. We can imagine that this end will be accomplished in different ways.

First, we imagine that wishing for what we want will stimulate the source of what is good to provide it to us. Wishing constitutes an essentially passive orientation toward satisfaction, and in this it is the opposite of work. We wish to gain the attention and care of the source of satisfaction. Power lies outside of us, except in the primitive sense that we may imagine a power in wishing itself. Wishing appeals to a higher power, and leads us to wait for that power to act. Wishing is the stance typical of an individual who does not imagine him or her self a center of initiative, who has lost the earlier sense of power over satisfaction associated with the infantile illusion described by Winnicott. When we wish for something, we do not take the initiative in seeking to acquire it for ourselves, but hope we will have it provided for us without our doing anything. Thus, not only is wishing the opposing pole to work, it is also the opposing pole to creativity and freedom.

If satisfaction is not forthcoming as a result of our wish, we must do something.[5] But it matters whether by doing something we mean somehow provoking the source of satisfaction to part with the goods it has created and now holds, or whether the failure of wishing provokes us to give up the idea that goods come from an object who holds them and must be made somehow to part with them. These two options correspond to two kinds of work: alienated labor for another to secure the means of satisfaction, and labor as the expression of freedom.

---

[5] An alternative is that we might simply live in hope that our wish will be granted in the future.

It needs to be emphasized that in the first construction, the holder of what is good is itself good insofar as it satisfies, and bad insofar as it does not. The assumption that the other holds the good means that whether we are satisfied or not is always a matter of the will of the other who holds the power over the goods we desire to have for our selves. When the holder of the goods provides them to us, the holder is itself good; it is, in psychoanalytic language, a "good object." The fact that it satisfies us sponsors the development in us of a positive emotional investment. It is the good object because it is the object or target of our positive feelings, of love and hope. When the imagined holder of the good does not provide it to us, we imagine that it withholds the good from us, keeps it for itself. We then experience the holder of the goods we desire as a bad object, as the target of our anger and hate.

What we need to secure satisfaction, then, is the good object. In primitive emotional development, failure to find satisfaction means the absence of this object and its replacement by the bad object. When satisfaction is understood as acquiring what we desire from another who has it, the problem of work and satisfaction is understood as the problem of finding, securing, and protecting the good object.

### Alienated labor

Work becomes necessary when we realize that satisfaction does not come to us merely because we desire it or wish for it, but only when we do something to acquire it. It still matters, however, how we conceive the doing that produces the goods that satisfy our desire. In other words, work can still take on different meanings. These meanings are linked to the modalities of work outlined above. Central to understanding the emerging significance of work is the transition from the state of dependence to one of separate being and how that transition affects the infantile illusion of creative power. How does the child experience and understand the existence of a separate reality in which he or she must seek satisfaction? Is it conceived as a simple extension of the primitive state of dependence in which need produces satisfaction by its own power? That is, does the adult continue to conceive satisfaction as an entitlement? Is the adult world conceived as one that mirrors the infantile relation in which the object that satisfies desire is held by a higher power conceived on the model of the parent who demands the child adapt to his or her need, and who must be induced to part with what the child wants? Finally, is the adult world conceived as a place in which a productive interaction can develop between an inner creative power, which is the heir to the infantile illusion of omnipotence, and an external reality it can affect but not control?

All of these alternatives can be thought about as lying along a continuum defined by the locus and nature of the human creative power and its relationship to work. Does human creative power reside in the individual and get expressed in work? Does human creative power reside in the individual but not in a form requiring him or her to work, so that it mirrors the illusion of creative power of the infant, who did not need to work to gain satisfaction? Or does human creative power reside outside the individual, in others or in an apparatus of production, so that work is disconnected from it, and the worker does nothing creative when he or she works?

Poverty bears a special relation to each of these constructions. Where the second predominates, poverty is a likely outcome, since, unless the individual has the good fortune to find him or her self in a situation that affirms the illusion that desire produces satisfaction, the construction stands in the way of work, whether creative or not. The sense of entitlement stands in the way of the individual working, and especially, learning the skill needed to do creative work, since, within the terms of this construction, neither work nor skill are needed for the creative act. Here, wealth is the means society provides a few of its members to keep alive the primitive illusion that desire produces its own satisfaction.

Where the third construction predominates, work means unskilled labor, which is routinized, manual labor in which the element of thinking is minimized. Because the skill is outside the worker, the worker does not and cannot direct the production process, which is a process in which he or she is not the subject, but simply one of the material inputs. In this construction, work is a means for acquiring what we desire, though it is not the creative act that produces what we desire. Of course, it may contribute something to that act, but the something it contributes is not creativity in doing. In this construction, as it comes down to us from the classical economists, the worker works for money. The loss of the primitive illusion of creative power is here more or less complete. Work is in no sense the heir to that illusion; it does not represent adaptation of that illusion to a reality in which satisfaction must be sought in relations with others we do not control. Rather, work represents the loss of the illusion. We work for money, which we use to buy what we can of the goods we need and desire.

Emotionally, this suggests the following construction: what we desire is money. Money is not produced by our work, but work is what we do to get the owner of the money to part with it. When the goods we desire, or the money needed to acquire them, are held by another, who will not part with them merely because we wish him or her to, then we must work to get them, which is to say we must subordinate ourselves to the source of satisfaction to acquire what we want. We work not to produce the goods we desire, but to get the holder of those goods to part with them. We work for the other. We do this when we work for money, and when acquiring the money paid to us for our work is the only or primary source of satisfaction in work. The money enables us to buy at least some of what we need, while work enables those who have money to have what they need produced, which is the profit from the sale of work's product.

In this relationship of working for another, work can have different meanings depending on whether we retain the idea that the other is the good object, or give that up in favor of the idea that the other is essentially a bad object. The difference has to do with how we allocate responsibility for the fact that the object does not provide us with what we need simply because we need it. Is it because the object is intent on withholding what we need for itself, or is it because we do not deserve to have what we need? Is the object bad, or are we? Another possibility is that the object has for some reason lost its capacity to provide satisfaction, a result we might imagine we have caused by demanding too much from it. Then our need has exhausted the object and left it unable to satisfy us. If we construct our relationship along these lines, we might draw the conclusion that the route to satisfaction is to repair the object. Then, work has the psychological meaning of repair or reparation.[6] The idea of work as repair or reparation links to notions of work as sacrifice or service. Work conceived in this way is an activity of self-negation and submission to a higher good, whether that be the good of the community or the will of God.

Work now takes on an emotional significance exactly the opposite of that associated with the expression of creative power. When our work expresses our creative power, and translates the infantile illusion into adult terms, work is an expression of our original vitality, our true self. It is, in this sense, an affirmation of self. But, when work is done to atone for the harm we have, or imagine we have, done, when an important part of its driving force is guilt and the reparative urge, then work is a negation of the self. It is an expression of hate for the self and of the need that the self be suppressed in favor of serving the needs of others.

So long as we imagine the source of satisfaction as the holder of the good, whatever work we do is not to produce the good, but to make ourselves worthy to receive it. Once, however, we come to realize that

---

[6] On the psychology of repair and reparation, see Klein (1937).

the other does not hold the good we desire, another possibility develops, the possibility that through work we can ourselves produce the good. What enables the other to continue to get us to work when we have come to realize that it is work that produces goods and not work that makes us worthy to receive them? The answer has to do with the elements of work. The other may not hold the good, but he may hold the secret to its production, the knowledge needed if work is to eventuate in anything good. Holding knowledge means concretely holding the idea of the good in the form of a process of its creation, and in that sense, we can say that the object does not hold the goods, but holds the creative power required to produce them. All that we can do is to assist the object in whatever way is needed for us to merit receipt of a share of the goods created with this power. Thus what is alienated in alienated labor is the creative power.

What this means concretely is that the object holds the knowledge of the technique and the means of production in which that technique is embodied. On our side, we remain incapable of producing anything since we do not know how to do so and do not have the necessary means. Knowing how to produce something is what we mean by having a skill, so we can say that our lack of skill means that we lack the power to create, and our lack of skill means that we must do the bidding of the object that possesses that power. The result of this is what Marx refers to as alienated labor, which is labor alienated from the subjectivity of the laborer (Levine 2001: 46–48, 93–96). While Marx sometimes identifies alienation of labor with formal ownership so that alienation means that the worker does not own his or her product, he also considers alienation a more basic condition of labor that does not express the laborer's subjectivity, which would apply whether the laborer owned the product or not. The two meanings of alienation (one linked to ownership, the other to the intrinsic character of the work) are in some ways connected, but it is primarily the latter that we have in mind here. Alienated labor understood as labor that implies for the worker the "loss of himself" (Marx 1977b: 80) is labor in which the worker does not exercise a skill, since to exercise a skill means to combine freedom with work.

In most cases, the inability to do skilled labor is not an original defect in the laborer's natural endowment, but a result of the failure of an original potential to develop into a capability to do something. When this capability does not develop, it becomes natural to assume that a creative power we might have found inside exists, and only can exist, outside, that it resides in the object. We hold to this assumption because we are unworthy of being containers for human creativity. We may feel unworthy because *a priori* considerations, for example of race or gender, are used to make us feel unworthy, in which case we can be said to be excluded by an externally given definition of our selves. But, if we internalize this definition, turn it into a self-conception, then we remain unworthy regardless of the legal protections we enjoy that assure our access to the means for learning the skills that would unite within us our power to work and our power to create. Then, we become unable to learn a skill because we do not imagine ourselves a creative source, and because we consider ourselves unworthy of holding any true creative power.

For those who cannot learn a skill, three options remain available. First, they may give up any hope for satisfaction, and turn away from desire in the direction of hate and despair. Second, they may remain at the level of the wish, so that, unable to be the source of satisfaction, they stand in wait for the arrival of that source and its benevolence toward them. They wish for satisfaction from a hoped–for omnipotent source that holds the means rather than producing it. This represents a regression to, or failure to develop beyond, the most primitive modality of the relationship of satisfaction. Third, they may go to work for an object that holds the creative power they lack so that they can receive that meager allotment of satisfaction due those who cannot create, and therefore remain unfree: their subsistence.

*Part III*

### The facilitating environment and the normative order

In this book, we treat poverty as the lack of something vital in living. We consider this something vital the capacity and opportunity to make doing the expression of being. The availability of the capacity depends on a number of factors, the most important of which fall into the category Winnicott refers to as a "facilitating environment." In concluding, we would like to explore this dimension of the problem in a preliminary way to indicate what our concept of poverty might imply for policy and institutions.

The literature directly concerned with the facilitating environment tends to conceive it narrowly as the environment in the family, and especially the relationships that shape early emotional development. If we were to summarize the issue at this level, the main elements would be (1) the conception of the emerging person held in the mind of the parent, especially whether that conception is animated by the principle of the "freedom of opportunities yet undetermined" as Erikson terms it, and (2) the provision of a setting in which it is safe to make doing an expression of being so that it is possible for self-development to occur.

We can make our main point in the following way. The parent relates to the infant or young child in a specific way, shaping a relationship that has a specific meaning into which the infant or young child fits. We can divide the modes of relating into two groups. In one, the parent already knows the shape of the life to come that is only beginning for the child. In the other, the parent does not know that shape of life, and relates to the child as an incipient person yet to be determined. In the second mode of relating, the parent takes an interest in and provides a safe environment for the child's developing self; in the first, the parent fails to do so either by directly attacking the child's impulse to self-development, or by treating that impulse as of no importance.

Thus, the parent may presume to know ahead of time the child's talents and interests, character structure, and emotional capacities. The parent may, for example, assume the child will turn out like the parent, or like the parent wishes he or she was. Alternatively, the parent may make no assumptions about character, talent, and interest, but, instead, adapt to the inclinations exhibited by the developing child, and provide that development with a facilitating environment. The parent may presume to know the child before the child makes his or her self known, or the parent may make no such presumption.

In a true facilitating environment, the parent does not reject the child's self-development, but rather places a significant value on it. In the absence of a facilitating environment, the child's task is to adapt to life in a world ill suited to being a self and where doing cannot be made an expression of being. In Winnicott's language this is the path of compliance. Along this path, the parent's need for the child to relate in a particular way displaces any need original to the child. Put too simply, it is what the parent needs that governs the relationship, and the child's need will only be satisfied so far as doing so serves the parent's need. In such cases, one of the parent's greatest needs is for the child to follow an expected development at the end of which is a shape of life well adapted to the parent's needs and expectations.

Though compelling on its own terms, thinking about the parent–child relationship in this way tends to conceive the interpersonal world of the family in isolation. It ignores how the way in which the parent relates to the child expresses societal ideals translated into norms of family life. Thus, our picture of childhood development should be adjusted to include the dominance of the family relationship by ideals that do not originate there. These ideals exist as modes of relatedness rather than as consciously held values; and, indeed, the norm of relatedness may even conflict with the values articulated in the larger community. In understanding the problem of development it is not, then, to the articulated values of the community that we need to turn, but to the values implicit in the norms of interaction. The parent–child relationship is shaped and determined by an ideal or set of ideals instantiated into these norms as modes of relatedness. The parents, whether consciously aware or not, act as conduits through which prevailing ideals are transmitted across generations.

When the norms of relatedness within the family express ideals other than those of self-development, they express ideals linked to compliance with others and with the expectations of the community or group. The alternative, as we have emphasized, is the upbringing not of a member, but of an individual. For this to take place, the facilitating environment must have an appropriate shape, which is to say, it must be governed by a suitable ideal. This is the ideal of the life not already determined, as expressed in needs not already known. The idea of needs not already known is the central idea in our conception of poverty. It requires that we re-conceive poverty on a basis other than the lack of subsistence and of the ability to live the prescribed life.

While the matter of the upbringing of an individual is a complex one, in essence it is simple enough. The parents must provide an environment for the child in which not knowing who the child will be is the essential determining element, and concern for the child's unique pattern of self-development is the guiding principle. As Winnicott puts it, "the parents do not have to make their baby as the artist has to make his picture or the potter his pot. The baby grows in his or her own way if the environment is good enough" (1965: 96). For this to happen, the child's need for self-development must dominate in the relationship. Dominance of self-development as a goal is, then, the ideal that organizes family life so far as the child is concerned. This ideal may or may not be consciously applied. Whether the ideal is consciously applied or not, its presence as the governing principle of family life assures that the capacity to make doing an expression of being can develop.

In Chapter 5, we considered how poverty can result from the loss of the ability to make a positive investment in the self due to the dominance of an ascribed and denigrated identity. The ascribed identity is one imposed on the individual from outside and in the service of others. Ascribed identity is, then, closely linked with the parent's failure to provide a facilitating environment, and with the parent's effort to replace the facilitating environment with one in which the parent's needs are imposed on the child. Ascribed identity is also closely linked to the denigration of the self, which must be replaced as the center of initiative with an external source of meaning in life and an external determination of conduct. This external determination is what we refer to above as compliance. Indeed, compliance requires self-repression, and in this sense requires that being your self cannot be invested with a positive value. If we cannot invest being our selves with a positive value, we cannot make doing the expression of being, which means that we cannot be a creative center.

Ascribed identity and the denigration of the self can be understood as the transmission of societal ideals through the vehicle of family relations. The mechanisms outlined by Winnicott operate as devices for the inter-generational transmission of impoverishment, which is the condition of having a devalued self and an ascribed identity inconsistent with being a center of initiative. To block the transmission process, it is necessary to block the impulse to impose an identity on the child and treat the parent – child relationship as an opportunity to realize in the child an already known identity or otherwise deny the child the opportunity to make and sustain a positive investment in his or her self.

Once we understand that the facilitating environment is shaped by ideals, and that the relationships within which the child develops are determined by the norms embodied in those ideals, we can also see how the problem of the development of the capacity for creative living depends on much more than the immediate relations within the family. It depends on the embedding of an ideal as the normative structure of a larger social order. Poverty in our sense results from the failure of the larger society to secure for some of those in it the positive investment in the self and the connected ideal of creative living as the governing norm of family life. Family failure expresses societal failure.

Yet, even where societal norms appropriate to creative living prevail, families may fail due to particular circumstances. Parents may not bring an adequate endowment of emotional capability to the task of raising children. Parents may become ill or die during the child's maturation period. In such cases, the inability to live independently may still result, and some will still be poor. But, it is not unreasonable to consider their poverty a local failing. Where, however, the ideal of creative living is not well embedded in family life because of the community's larger ambivalence about the ideal of the individual, the problem exists at the local level because of the hold that notions of living that incorporate the norm of compliance, or otherwise insist on self-repression, continue to have at the level of the community as a whole. Then, the problem is a societal problem, and requires change in institutions and policies. In the first instance, this means change in ideals that govern interaction at all levels, especially the level of the upbringing of children.

For this work to be done, however, we need to rethink the language typically used to discuss the embedding and changing of norms. Typically, in speaking of ideals we speak in the language of values, especially of teaching values. But, the key element in the idea of teaching values is adaptation to what already exists and to the predetermined expectations of a community. Compliance, however, is the antithesis of creativity in living, and this means that the idea of implanting values leads us in the wrong direction (Winnicott 1965).

## The problem of values

The objection may arise that without values and the connection to community they imply the individual cannot find meaning in life, or the connection with others that underpins the discovery of meaning in life. It might be further claimed that without this connection to community expressed in identification with the community's values, the individual must feel isolated and disconnected, with the likely result that he or she will turn away from others, fail to see in them fellows to be treated with concern and respect.

This objection rests on the premise that it is identification with the group that fosters regard for others, a premise we can question (Levine 1999b). After all, the opposition of self and other is built into group life, where concern is limited to those who are also members of our group, and with whom we are therefore identified. Arguments along the lines just suggested tend, therefore, to confuse the problem with the solution. Still, they do suggest that we consider how creative living as we have defined it does or does not foster connection with others.

In a moral order, connection with others is a matter of shared group identity and subordination of the individual self to the ways of life sanctioned by the group, ways of life that carry the meaning of group identification. By contrast, in a modern society connection with others has a different meaning. The basis of this meaning is not identification with, but recognition of, others (Winnicott 1971; Benjamin 1992). Unlike identification, which is, as Freud suggests, the earliest form of human connection (Freud 1959), recognition calls on capacities that only emerge later in the process of human emotional development.

We can understand the distinction between recognition and identification in the following way. Identification connects us to others along the dimension of shared qualities conceived concretely. Through identification, those in the group imagine themselves, and to a degree attempt to become, the same sort of person by leading the same sort of life. Recognition connects us to others who do not share the concrete qualities of character and way of life. In recognition, what we share are not the concrete characteristics associated with a particular way of life and way of being, but the abstract qualities associated with a general idea of being a person conceived independently of the realization of that idea in any particular concrete form.

Identification shapes the earliest of our relationships, which are the relationships with our caretakers, and more broadly with our family members. These familial and familial-type bonds hold together societal and subsocietal groups based on the principle of identification and significant sameness: ethnic groups, racial groups, gender groups, religious communities, and so on. Such connections are felt rather than thought, concrete rather than abstract, particular rather than universal. They are the bonds of shared ways of life, concretely considered.

Recognition, by contrast, calls on capacities for connection with others developed later in the maturation process, capacities that enable the individual to understand that his or her particular experience of having a self is not the only such experience, that humanness is not essentially a shared identity, but a shared capacity to shape an identity, that being human therefore does not mean conforming with a particular, concrete, way of life. To escape the equation of human with a particular shape that humanness can adopt requires that we see humanness as a potential rather than an already formed reality. In other words, it requires that we understand humanness, personhood, and self as ideas rather than as immediately and concretely lived experiences. This capacity for holding an idea capable of being realized in various ways is the capacity to recognize selfhood in others who are different, since it is possible for others to realize the ideal of self without living the same sort of life we do, or sharing the same goals, or valuing the same things.

To understand better the implications of the inability to exercise the capacity to conceive humanness in the abstract, as a potential rather than an already given reality, consider an example taken from the age of discovery, and from the most famous of discoverers, Christopher Columbus (see Levine 2002). What Columbus discovers, among other things, are the people of the New World. Todorov (1987) suggests that he discovers them not once, but twice, first as humans in his own image, second as something different from, and therefore less than, human. Since God made man in His own image, so far as man is the European of Columbus's time, that European represents God's image. Therefore, those made in that image are human, and those made in other than that image are not, or not fully, human. In other words, Columbus does not see humanness as a general matter, as a potential that might be realized in different ways; rather, he sees it concretely as something embedded in and inseparable from one particular way of being: language, religion, mode of dress, manner of relating, and so on.

If you cannot conceive different ways of being human, it is because your way of thinking lacks a general concept of humanness. Clearly, this was the case for Columbus, who equated being human with what we would, appealing to our general concept, treat as one instance or concrete form of humanness. The problem lies in the way he thinks about otherness and difference with regard to persons. The notion of difference demands access to the idea of a potential, which is to say, a universal, and his access here is severely limited.

The capacity to think in general terms, to conceive what might be rather than what already is, is closely linked to the ideal of creative living that we have made central to our conceptions of poverty and work. In that ideal, the key element is not an already known and concretely defined way of life, but the capacity to discover what is not already known. What takes on significance for the individual is not the customs and norms of the group, but this capacity and the freedom to exercise it. When this ideal takes on significance, regard for others becomes a real possibility. Regard for others really means regard for the self as a potential, and concern that it have a facilitating environment in which to develop. Because regard for this potential is essentially what we mean by regard for the self, self-regard and regard for others is the same thing, or, at least, it becomes the same thing once we begin to exercise our capacity to conceive the self in more abstract terms, as a potential rather than the shape of an already given reality.

The key element in this is that regard for the self becomes regard for others only so far as the self can be conceived in the abstract, as a potential. By contrast, regard for others conflicts with concern for the self when the self is conceived only concretely. Conceiving the self concretely means identifying with an already formed identity, especially a group identity. So, by submerging self into the group we assure that a more abstract idea of the self cannot develop, and regard for others will be impaired. The crucial element in the capacity to treat others with concern is not, then, the capacity to identify with or internalize values, or the related capacity to conceive of one's self within a group or community, but the capacity to think abstractly about the self, and to make an emotional investment in the idea of the self considered in the abstract, as a potential or capacity.

This conclusion calls into question programs designed to instill morally acceptable behavior through teaching or otherwise implanting values. Winnicott treats the impulse to implant values as an expression of impatience about development. This impatience expresses dissatisfaction with the development process on two related grounds. First, the development process is regulated within the child and not controlled by the parent, so patience really means the capacity to give up external control over the process. Second, the development process, because it is regulated within the child, has an end also determined within. The parent does not determine what the child will become, so the parent's impatience is really the expression of dissatisfaction with an outcome other than that prescribed for the child. If impatience is the attitude that distorts the development process, preventing it from proceeding at its own pace and to its own unique outcome, patience is the attitude of respect for the internal process of development, which is the same thing as respect for the autonomy of the child and of the person the child will become, given an environment conducive to the unfolding of the child's own development.

We cannot through policy force parents to adopt the attitude of patience toward, and tolerance of, development. Yet, tolerance of development is the key element in assuring that the adult emerging at the end of the development process will be capable of creative living, and therefore of creative work. While we cannot shape policies that assure the parent will adopt the appropriate attitude, we can identify the tolerance of development as the key ideal of a free society.

What stands in the way of tolerance of development is what Wilfred Bion refers to as the "hatred of a process of development." Hatred of the process of development expresses the wish to arrive "fully equipped as an adult fitted by instinct to know without training or development exactly how to live and move" (1961: 89). To learn a skill and do work requires just this training and development. It requires that we accept that we are not born fully equipped for adult life. The alternative to development, according to Bion, is to join a group of a particular kind. In this group, the problem of living is solved for the member, so no development is required. The individual needs no skill other than the ability to "sink his identity in the herd."

## The problem of change

How can we begin to translate the issues just raised from the level of individual psychology and personal development to the level of social institutions and policy? We can find the key to answering this question in the ideals that operate at both levels. If we understand that the parent–child relationship is about the intergenerational transmission of ideals that do not, however, originate in that relationship and are not unique to it, then we can understand the dependence of that relationship on a larger normative order. Change in the psychological configuration of family life is, then, an element of change in the normative order. So far as the conditions that impede development are the same conditions that recreate the normative order, the problem of development, and therefore the problem of poverty as we have conceived it, is a problem of change in that order.

We can conceive change in ideals in different ways. One applies where ideals are consciously known and held, and where commitment to them can be considered a decision made by an agent capable of making such a commitment. This conception of ideals considers them separate from the agent that has them. If this is the case, then change in ideals is a matter of choice, and the struggle over ideals a conscious engagement with alternatives. We may conceive this choice in different ways, for example as a matter of calculation of costs and benefits. However we conceive it, change is a struggle among stakeholders over which values will dominate.

All of this would hold if we could conceive the agent separately from the ideals to which he or she is committed, and if we could consider ideals essentially a matter of conscious knowledge and intent. Yet, so far as ideals are embedded in identity, we cannot readily assume the separation between agent and ideal required for treating the problem in this way. If we consider, as we have so far, that basic ideals fall under two headings – compliance and creativity – then our ideals are essentially orientations toward the self and its place in the world. They are not simply values chosen and adopted, but part of the essential make-up of the agent, especially of his or her identity. This has an important bearing on change.

If the agent to which we have just referred is a group member whose identity is organized around the idea of being in the group and sharing an identity with the group, then adherence to ideals has the same meaning as belonging to a group. The essential ideal is compliance with the group, which means adopting the beliefs shared in the group. Since the essential ideal is compliance, change is linked either to change in the group itself or to a movement from one group to another. That is, we can adhere to the ideal of compliance by subordinating ourselves to the group, whatever that group is and whatever are its constituting values (see Levine 1999b). We can change our consciously held values to adapt either to changes within our group or to the need to make a transition to another group because such change does not affect our underlying commitment to an ideal of compliance.

This possibility provides the underlying rationale for the notion that teaching values is the essential element in bringing about change, so that change can be taught, for example in the schools. It is also an attitude that makes schools a central battleground for social change. If poverty is the result of the failure to inculcate an appropriate ideal, the solution to the problem of poverty is to make sure the appropriate values are taught in the schools. This makes the school the center for moral education toward membership in a moral order rather than a part of the child's development of the capacity for creative living and of the skills needed to live independently in a world of independent persons. Rather than being the steward of the child's impulse to develop these skills, the school is the prize to be won in the struggle of groups over control of societal values and the ways of life that will and will not be sanctioned for members. Rather than providing the child with an extension of the facilitating environment of the family devoted to the child's development, the school collaborates with the family's role in self-repression by seeking to inculcate values.

This idea of change might work well enough so long as we operate within the ideal of compliance and our goal is to shift allegiance from one group to another, or within the group from one set of group-constituting values to another. The idea does not work where the problem is to shift allegiance from the ideal of compliance to the ideal of creativity, since by definition we cannot do so by calling on the individual's impulse to adapt his or her thinking to the group's expectations. What this change demands is not change in group values, or movement to a different group, but the capacity to live a life outside the group and in so doing to make life the expression of an ideal that reduces radically the hold the group has over its members. As a matter of policy, what this requires is attention to the individual as the end of policy, and especially to the individual conceived outside the group.[1]

The individual conceived outside the group is also the individual conceived outside the moral order, which is the order of group life, the order of identification with group-constituting values and compliance with the group's expectations. Poverty policy appropriate to an ideal of self-determination and creative living begins with the idea not of the group member, but of the individual, an ideal that can be realized to different degrees. Poverty policy appropriate to a free society begins, then, where the moral order ends.

## Poverty policy as development

To begin with the idea of the individual is to begin with the interrelated ideas of will, creativity, and self-determination. As we have seen, the idea of will and responsibility for self as the basis for conduct interpreted along the lines first suggested by the Puritans establishes the terms for the debate over poverty policy. The primary effect of this ideal has been to limit the scope of policy and to assure that the formulation of policy will involve a punitive element. Yet, however extreme and one-sided the appeal to will as the ideal to be achieved, we will not get far if we treat the matter of policy as one that can be well formulated without reference to the concerns that the ideal of will brings to the fore.

This will be clear if we consider once again the matter of the capability for creativity in work and living we have here suggested should be our primary objective in shaping social institutions. The ideal of creativity does not, after all, stand opposed to will, but shares with it a vital implication: poverty means a failure of autonomy and self-determination.

---

[1] Anna Yeatman explores one approach to shaping a social policy consistent with commitment to individual self-determination as the governing ideal. She suggests that we speak of welfare in the language of "individualized service delivery," the point being that public services target individuals, and, so far as possible, conceive of the recipients of public services as individuals rather than group members (Yeatman 2003).

We can consider this failure both objectively, as a failure of institutions, and subjectively, as a failure of individual capability.

We have suggested that the ability to live creatively is a product of the development of an original potential into a capability. This development occurs when the individual finds him or her self in a facilitating environment, one conducive to the expression of the creative impulse, rather than one that leads the individual to repress that impulse and substitute for it an identity organized on the basis of compliance. The problem for poverty policy, then, is essentially the problem of development. In other words, the link between development and freedom (Levine 1995; Sen 1999), freedom and creativity, creativity and skill, and between poverty and the lack of skill, means that the goal of poverty policy should be to promote development, both at the level of the individual and at the level of the society as a whole.

When we limit our understanding of poverty to levels of consumption and the availability of subsistence somehow defined, the problem of poverty policy becomes simpler: how do we assure that all citizens have adequate access to the means of subsistence, and how do all countries provide this access to their citizens? Traditional approaches to poverty policy operate within this construction so far as their emphasis is on transfer payments and the provision of welfare for the needy. If we think of poverty as the failure to develop the capacity for creative living, however, such measures are not so much the solution to the problem of poverty as they are ways we can make living with poverty more tolerable. Making living with poverty more tolerable can be an important and worthwhile goal. In some cases it is the best we can do. But, more may be possible, though the measures required are more complex than are the measures needed simply to alleviate the suffering poverty imposes on the poor.

The problem of poverty policy becomes more difficult when we consider the links between poverty and capability and between capability and development. Development is not, after all, a policy, though some might argue that it is the result of the application of appropriate policy. Even if development might be promoted by some policies and impeded by others, however, this does not mean that government can make it happen at will. This is especially the case for development whose end is not wealth, or even wealth per capita, but the capacity for creative living and, in this sense, freedom.

Because compliance as the opposing pole to creative living is so closely associated with group life, poverty policy as development involves reconceiving the role of the group in shaping identity and determining life experience. This is no easy matter, since it requires that the group

member give up the comfort and security of the group for the uncertainty of a life of creativity and discovery. It means sacrificing the
assurance of who we are that is provided by group identity for the work
of discovering and taking on an individual identity that includes identification with a vocation and the skill associated with it. It requires learning
a skill and making an emotional investment in the idea of the self as
doing skilled work.

This can only happen when the alternative ceases to be positively
valued as an important source of security and of meaning in life. The
individual cannot accomplish this disinvestment from the group by
him or her self. The problem of poverty policy as development, then,
is to provide the individual with a supportive or facilitating environment. A solution to this problem is what we will refer to as stewardship
and the stewardship role of the public authority. We conclude with a
brief suggestion of how we might understand stewardship with special
reference to rights, and the role of the public authority as the steward of
right.

### Rights, welfare, and stewardship

In offering some possibilities for addressing the problem of poverty, we
do not emphasize the language of rights, or suggest that right should be
central to the formulation of policy. Given the emphasis we have placed
on the idea of right, and especially on the notion of freedom that right
institutes in law and policy, it may seem odd that we do not speak of
policy in the language of right. The reasons for this are important and
have to do with the complex relationship between right and the problem
of poverty.[2]

The problem with applying the language of right to poverty policy is
that it assumes a condition whose absence is implied in the state of being
poor. That is, the language of right assumes the capacity for agency and
will, which is the capacity to make doing an expression of being. But, for
those who are poor due to impairment in their capacity for creative
living, this is an assumption we cannot make. For them, doing can only
in a limited sense be considered an expression of will. Yet, without will
there can be no meaningful exercise of right. The factors that limit the
application of the language of will equally limit the application of the
language of right.

This conclusion applies most notably to the assertion that there are
rights to satisfy needs, an idea that comes into direct conflict with the

---

[2] For a fuller discussion of some of the issues considered in this section, see Levine (2001).

idea of will as the capacity to suspend need. The capacity to suspend need is the starting point for the development of needs not already known and determined; it is the entry point to the world of creative living. To have a right to satisfy need makes right derive from the intensity of need, and insists on the domination of need over will. Will, rather than being the gateway to needs not already determined, becomes instead the means to assert need and assure that already determined needs (for food, shelter, health care, and so on) will be satisfied. To insist that the poor have a right to the things they need, and the acquisition of which will take them out of poverty, is to deny the condition of poverty.

These considerations lead us to the following question: Is there another way to think about the problem of welfare that is consistent with the spirit of the ideal of rights, but does not require us to apply that ideal in ways inconsistent with it? One possible answer to this question appeals to the idea of capability. If we think of will not simply as an action, but as a capability, then it is possible to consider how that capability develops. And, it is possible to consider how individuals might fail to one degree or another in the effort to acquire the capability, and because of this how they may fail to live creatively. The language that describes the failure to gain the capability to suspend need and to tolerate the state of not knowing is the language of impairment. Those with impaired capabilities cannot live independently in a world designed for the exercise of will. They need assistance in doing so.

It can be argued that we all spend at least a part of our lives in this state of need and dependence. Early in life we are radically dependent on our parents, and, even as we mature, through childhood and adolescence, we still lack a fully formed capacity for autonomous living, and thus for the full exercise of right. Later in life, we may find our capacities impaired for a greater or lesser period due to illness. As we age, the likelihood of impairment increases, and many individuals find themselves once again in a state of dependence. Thus, the experience of impairment is not limited to a part of society, though at any given time only some will be impaired. Accepting these conclusions, we can begin to see what it is the welfare state needs to do that is both consistent with the spirit of rights, but yet not quite the implementation of rights.

If the capability to act at our will is not simply present or absent, but always subject to a greater or lesser degree of impairment, then the problem of institutions is not simply to offer protection for the already developed capacity to exercise right, but also to facilitate both the development of the capability and its exercise to the degree that the individual is capable. The protection of right is not, then, an either/or matter, as would be implied by the policy that requires that the government do no more than protect or implement rights. The capabilities language enables us to consider the matter of rights and government obligations in a context where matters of degree are important.

The treatment of self-determination as a capability implies that it will not always be present, that if it is present it may be in some ways impaired, and that therefore all citizens cannot be assumed capable of making use of it under all circumstances and at all times. This means that the government cannot simply treat those in need of its services as individuals, fully capable of acting by and for themselves. To deal with this problem, we suggest conceiving the government as taking on a stewardship role. In this role, the agency responsible for welfare, the welfare state or public authority, acts not as an institution of governance or of representation, but as a steward responsible for protecting the freedom of those incapable of fully protecting and exercising their freedoms on their own.

The idea of stewardship points us in a direction different from governance. Governance imposes ends, and rules conduct in accordance with imposed ends. In a moral order, those in the community are subject to the imposition of ends first by those ranked above them, but ultimately by a divine authority. In the modern world, rule must, at least ideally, be self-rule. Self-rule may refer to the ideal of individual self-determination, in which case governance means self-governance: individuals determining their conduct in accord with their own ends. Self-rule may also refer to the collective or association, which sets agreed-upon limits for conduct and pursues ends individuals cannot achieve when acting on their own. We can use the term governance at both levels, but only so far as at each level there exists an agent competent to govern in a way consistent with the ideal of self-determination rather than the ideal of subjection to the rule of an external authority.

Even where such an agent exists, governance is not the only, or even the primary, concept we would want to apply to the work of a public authority in a free society. In such a society, rights and the attendant duties to respect rights regulate conduct. The authority responsible for securing rights does not govern, since it does not impose ends of its own, however determined. On the contrary, rights can be said to limit governance. Because securing rights is not an instance of rule, it already points us away from governance, and in the direction of what we refer to as stewardship.

So far as the steward does not govern those for whom it is responsible, stewardship can be distinguished from governance. In the case of the impaired, we cannot assume agency fully adequate to exercise right and make doing an expression of being. Yet, the ideal of conduct remains that it be regulated internally rather than externally. This ideal implies that the individual's failure to develop fully a capacity for self-determination does not justify subjecting him or her to the rule of an external authority with its own ends. Clearly, there is a tension built into these conditions. This tension is managed effectively when the public authority seeks to create an environment in which self-determination can be exercised, and limits or regulates conduct only in the interests of that ideal. Then, we can say that the public authority acts as steward for self-determination.

Movement toward a stewardship ideal and away from the ideal of the public authority as a structure of governance is the starting point for effective poverty policy. The poor need neither to govern nor to be governed, but, rather, to find themselves in an environment in which, so far as possible, they can develop and exercise what capacities they can to live a creative life.

# Conclusion

### Definition and measurement of poverty

Our conception of poverty applies to a society committed to the ideal of freedom. Freedom means that individuals are able to determine the sorts of lives they lead rather than having their lives determined for them. When individuals are free in this sense, it is not known in advance what sort of lives they will have or what those lives will require. Then, when we try to define poverty, we cannot mean a lack of a predetermined set of goods or income. Ways of thinking that define poverty as a lack of subsistence goods or of goods that will suffice to address basic needs falter where needs are not predetermined.

Thus, attempts to apply these notions to modern societies character-ized by rapid transformation of needs, and by a breakdown of the hold of group norms on the shape of individual lives, are bound to fail. We see this failure in two broad areas. The first is the effort to define poverty by specifying a level of income separating the poor from the non-poor, as is done in the United States and has been tried elsewhere. The problem of freezing what is a fluid set of needs is seen in the crude method of coming up with a minimal food budget and multiplying by three. But even where the exact method differs, the need to revise repeatedly and fundamen-tally the method to calculate poverty lines shows the difficulties in the approach. These have become so apparent that in many European countries poverty lines have been abandoned, and purely distributional methods are now used to define poverty. There the poor are defined as those in the bottom quartile of the income distribution, as those earning a certain fraction of the median income, or by a related method. But the median or mean income has no normative standing and therefore pro-vides an arbitrary and unconvincing basis for thinking about poverty. The second area where the fixity of needs is presumed in order to define poverty and to try to alleviate it is in the use of basic needs in develop-ment policy. Here, too, it has been difficult to specify what individuals require, even at a basic level. The problem is not only that there are different and changing cultural standards, but also that we run up against the fluidity of modern society, and so defining basic needs become difficult or impossible.

If what the poor lack cannot be prescribed in advance, there does not seem to be any way to define poverty. The solution is to focus on what individuals can be or do rather than what they can have, on capabilities rather than commodities, as Sen puts it. Considering capability in relation to freedom, we focus attention on what individuals need to live successfully in a world organized around the ideal of freedom. Freedom is not just the absence of constraint. It requires individuals to discover and create their modes of life, which means that they must have the capacity to discover and create.

Following Winnicott, we locate the genesis of this capacity in the early maturational environment of childhood, recognizing, however, that the shape of the early environment reflects larger societal norms. We emphasize the way the parent holds the idea of the child, and the extent to which the parent–child relationship includes the predetermination of the child's future. The parent's ability to avoid prejudging the child's development expresses the societal commitment to indeterminacy, and therefore to creativity. Being creative means being able to let go, temporarily, of external determination, and to dwell in the realm of the unformed and things that have yet to take shape. To dwell within oneself in this way means that an individual is comfortable with him- or herself and does not have an overriding desire to cling to the security that external determination may provide. We call this in-dwelling the capacity to be. The creativity that may result from this process expresses itself in the world and so must be consistent with reality, indeed become a part of it. Thus the individual's creativity is an act in the world, what we call doing. In this sense, those who live creatively make doing an expression of being. From this point of view, we can see that avoiding poverty is a matter of self-development. By self-development we mean individual development, but also the development of institutions of society consistent with individual self-determination. Poverty policy is thus development policy.

The doing that expresses being according to a norm of freedom is what we call work. This is a broad definition of work: work may be paid or unpaid; it is not confined to particular areas of endeavor. Since creativity must express itself in the world, creative living requires the acquisition of skill. In our way of thinking about skill, we have in mind not the acquisition of ways to routinize tasks, but the capacity to discover creative solutions to problems that cannot be solved by the routine application of already known technique. In order for skill to be useful in work that expresses creativity, the problems faced in work must be reasonably complex and engaging, and the worker must have discretion in seeking solutions. Thus, there are types of work that allow creativity to be expressed, and types of work that are routine, dull, and directed by rules or authority in a rigid way. This suggests that poverty may result not only from the failure of development of creative capacity, but also from inadequate opportunities to exercise it. Thus, our conception connects with the more usual notion of poverty being caused by inadequate opportunities for work. Our own contribution complements this approach, but we emphasize that it matters what kind of work the individual is capable of doing and has the opportunity to do.

This way of thinking means that the usual ways of measuring poverty do not address important aspects of the problem. If poverty must be seen in the context of needs that cannot be prescribed, then approaches relying on quantities of goods, poverty lines, or the capability to take part in specified activities do not address the problem. These approaches do have the advantage that they can provide objective measures, whereas to conceive poverty as the inadequate development of a capacity for creative living does not provide any simple solution to the problem of measurement. While this may be so, the emphasis on work and skill does suggest possible ways of measuring poverty. Thus poverty is likely to be less of a problem the greater are (1) the numbers of people educated in a way that develops skills providing the ability to solve general problems that require going beyond routine, and (2) the availability of work that is complex, engaging, and involves discretion. Thus while we cannot expect our idea of poverty to provide a simple measure, we can expect that some of its aspects can be measured.

### The norm of freedom

While we acknowledge that the norm of freedom is not universally held, it is nonetheless important. As we have suggested, the prevalence of this norm affects the way children are brought up. Thus the incidence of poverty does depend on the type of society in which individuals find themselves. This might lead one to conclude that poverty is a matter of circumstance. While poverty does have to do with circumstance, it is not only a matter of circumstance. A life that avoids poverty involves discovery and creativity, and these depend on the capacity for in-dwelling. As a result of this capacity, an individual will fashion a life for him- or herself. To the extent that the individual is expected to shape his or her life, and is given the opportunity to do so, the capacity to make doing an expression of will takes on significance. But, the exercise of will depends on both circumstance and capability, which means that in thinking about poverty we must reject not only the idea that will is all and circumstance nothing, but equally the idea that makes circumstance all and will nothing.

Since we avoid an emphasis on will as the sole determinant of the plight of the poor, we also avoid the long and corrosive tradition of blaming the poor for their fate. This leads us to reject the simplistic view that government programs cause poverty. Once we accept that the capacity to act at our will is not inborn, but requires a specific development, we can no longer assume that what people do must express will or its narrower derivatives such as rational calculation in the sense made popular by neoclassical economists. At the same time, while our conception of the problem allows significant space for government programs, especially to alleviate the suffering caused by poverty, we cannot assume that government has the power to solve the problem of poverty through policy. This is because of the link between poverty and development. Unless we make the doubtful assumption that development is the direct result of appropriate policy, we must accept that there are limits to what government can do, without thereby embracing the extreme view that government has no part to play, or is essentially a part of the problem.

We can understand something of the proper role of government with regard to the problem of poverty by considering it in relation to the individual's developmental needs, especially where those have not been adequately met in the past, so that the development to autonomy remains incomplete. This suggests a close link between the ends of parenting and those of government so far as the problem of capability is concerned. Just as good parenting facilitates rather than determines, and allows rather than forces the child to develop, good government provides opportunities, education, and stewardship. The goal is freely determined lives for individuals, rather than the maintenance or provision of a certain level of living. In this sense, our idea that poverty policy is development policy continues past childhood and the realm of the family into the realm of government and its responsibility for stewardship. Poverty policy is thus about seeing lives as belonging to individuals; what is important about these lives is not the level of income that they enjoy but that they are freely determined in a way that allows creative living in the world.

Poverty policy, given that it should be addressed to individuals, misses the point if it is aimed at groups. We have emphasized that the norm of freedom means that externally determined identities should not be imposed on individuals. We saw this as a problem in child rearing. To the extent individuals are ascribed membership in groups, their self-determination must be impaired. This does not mean that individuals may not choose to identify with groups, but only that doing so is a choice and not a matter of ascribed identity. Individual identity is primarily an individual matter.

# References

Allardt, E. (1978), "The Relationship between Objective and Subjective Measures in the Light of Comparative Study," in R. F. Tomassen (ed.), *Comparative Studies of Sociology*, vol. I (Greenwich, CT: JAI Press).

Andrews, F. M., and S. B. Withey (1976), *Social Indicators of Well-Being: Americans' Perceptions of Life Quality* (New York: Plenum Press).

Argyle, M. (2001), *The Psychology of Happiness*, 2nd edn (New York: Routledge).

Argyle, M., Martin, M. M., and J. Crossland (1989), "Happiness as a Function of Personality and Social Encounters," in J. P. Forgas and J. M. Innes (eds.), *Recent Advances in Social Psychology: An International Perspective* (Amsterdam: North-Holland: 189–203).

Argyris, C. (1990), *Overcoming Organizational Defenses: Facilitating Organizational Learning* (Boston: Allyn and Bacon).

Aristotle (1984), *Nicomachean Ethics*, in *The Complete Works of Aristotle*, vol. II, Trans. W. D. Ross (Princeton: Princeton University Press).

Beier, A. L. (1985), *Masterless Men: The Vagrancy Problem in England, 1560–1640* (Oxford: Oxford University Press).

Benjamin, J. (1992), "Recognition and Destruction: An Outline of Intersubjectivity," in N. Skolnick and S. Warshaw (eds.), *Relational Perspectives in Psychoanalysis* (Hillsdale, NJ: The Analytic Press).

Bentham, J. (1954), *Bentham's Economic Writings*, vol. III, W. Stark (ed.) (London: Royal Economic Society).

Berkowitz, L., C. Fraser, F. P. Treasure, and S. Cochran (1987), "Pay Equity, Job Qualifications, and Comparison in Pay Satisfaction," *Journal of Applied Psychology* 72: 544–551.

Berman, M. (1982), *All That Is Solid Melts into Air* (New York: Simon and Schuster).

Bion, W. (1961), *Experiences in Groups and Other Essays* (London: Tavistock).

Bird, E. J. (1998), "Politics, Altruism and the Definition of Poverty," Working Paper, University of Rochester.

Bollas, C. (1989), *Forces of Destiny* (London: Free Association Books).

Bourne, E. (1978), "The State of Research on Ego Identity: A Review and Appraisal. Part I," *Journal of Youth and Adolescence* 7: 223–251.

Braverman, H. (1974), *Labor and Monopoly Capital* (New York: Monthly Review Press).

Braybrooke, D. (1987), *Meeting Needs* (Princeton: Princeton University Press).

Bruner, J. (1962), *On Knowing* (Cambridge, MA: Harvard University Press).

Campbell, A. (1981), *The Sense of Well-Being in America* (New York: McGraw-Hill).

Campbell, A., E. Converse, and W. L. Rodgers (1976), *The Quality of American Life* (New York: Sage).

Chacko, T. I. (1983), "Job and Life Satisfaction: A Causal Analysis of their Relationships," *Academy of Management Journal* 26: 163–169.

Chan, R., and S. Joseph (2000), "Dimensions of Personality, Domains of Aspiration, and Subjective Well-Being," *Personality and Individual Differences* 28: 347–354.

Citro, C. F., and R. T. Michael (eds.) (1995), *Measuring Poverty: A New Approach* (Washington, DC: National Academy Press).

Clark, A. E., and A. J. Oswald (1996), "Satisfaction and Comparison Income," *Journal of Public Economics* 61: 359–381.

Clark, M. (1990), "Meaningful Social Bonding as a Universal Human Need," in J. Burton (ed.), *Conflict: Human Needs Theory* (New York: St. Martin's Press).

Clinton, W. J. (1998), "State of the Union,"

Dean, Mitchell (1991), *The Constitution of Poverty: Toward a Genealogy of Liberal Governance* (New York: Routledge).

Deane, Phyllis (1978), *The Evolution of Economic Ideas* (Cambridge: Cambridge University Press).

Debreu, G. (1959), *Theory of Value* (New York: Wiley).

Deci, E. L. (1975), *Intrinsic Motivation* (New York: Plenum Press).

Diener, E. (1984), "Subjective Well-Being," *Psychological Bulletin* 95: 542–575.

Diener, E., and S. Oishi (2002), "Money and Happiness: Income and Subjective Well-Being Across Nations," in E. Diener and E. M. Suh (eds.), *Subjective Well-Being Across Cultures* (Cambridge, MA: MIT Press).

Diener, E., and E. M. Suh (1997), "Measuring the Quality of Life: Economic, Social and Subjective Indicators," *Social Indicators Research* 40: 189–216.

Diener, E., M. Diener, and C. Diener (1995), "Factors Predicting The Subjective Well-Being of Nations," *Journal of Personality and Social Psychology* 69: 851–864.

Diener, E., R. A. Emmons, R. J. Larsen, and S. Griffin (1985), "The Satisfaction with Life Scale," *Journal of Personality Assessment* 49: 71–75.

Diener, E., E. M. Suh, R. E. Lucas, and H. L. Smith (1999), "Subjective Well-Being: Three Decades of Progress," *Psychological Bulletin* 125: 276–302.

Dittmar, H. (1992), *The Social Psychology of Material Possessions* (Hemel Hempsted: Harvester Wheatsheaf).

Douglas, M., D. Gasper, S. Ney, and M. Thompson (1998), "Human Needs and Wants," in S. Rayner and E. L. Malone (eds.), *Human Choice and Climate Change, Vol. 1: The Societal Framework* (Columbus, OH: Battelle Press: 195–263).

Easton, L., and K. Guddat (1967), *Writings of the Young Marx on Philosophy and Society* (Garden City, NY: Doubleday).

Eden, F. M. (1968[1797]), *The State of the Poor* (New York: Augustus M. Kelley).

Edwards, R. (1979), *Contested Terrain: The Transformation of the Work Place in the Twentieth Century* (New York: Basic).

Eigen, M. (1996), *Psychic Deadness* (Northvale, NJ: Jason Arsonson).

Erikson, E. (1956), "The Problem of Ego Identity," *Journal of the American Psychoanalytic Association* 4: 58–121.

(1980[1959]), *Identity and the Life Cycle* (New York: W. W. Norton).

(1964), *Insight and Responsibility* (New York: W. W. Norton).

Fisher, G. (1997), "The Development and History of the US Poverty Thresholds – A Brief Overview," *Newsletter of the Government Statistics Section and the Social Statistics Section of the American Statistical Association*: 6–7.

Form, W. (1981), "Resolving Ideological Issues on the Division of Labor," in Hubert M. Blalock, Jr. (ed.), *Theory and Research in Sociology* (New York: Free Press).

Freedman, N. (1980), "Splitting and its Resolution," *Psychoanalysis and Contemporary Thought* 3: 237–266.

French, R., and P. Simpson (1999), "Our Best Work Happens When We Don't Know What We're Doing," *Socio-Analysis* 1: 216–230.

Freud, S. (1959), *Group Psychology and the Analysis of the Ego* (New York: W. W. Norton).

Furniss, E. S. (1920/1957), *The Position of the Laborer in a System of Nationalism: A Study in the Labor Theories of the Later Mercantilists* (New York: Augustus M. Kelley).

Galbraith, J. K. (1958), *The Affluent Society* (Boston: Houghton Mifflin).

Gallie, D., M. White, Y. Cheng, and M. Tomlinson (1998), *Restructuring the Employment Relationship* (Oxford: Clarendon).

Gellner, E. (1983), *Nations and Nationalism* (Ithaca: Cornell University Press).

Geremek, B. (1994), *Poverty: A History* (Oxford: Blackwell).

Ghislen, B. (1954), *The Creative Process* (New York: Mentor Books).

Gingrich, N. (1995), *To Renew America* (New York: HarperCollins).

Green, R. (1976), "Basic Human Needs," *IDS Bulletin* 9: 7–11.

Greenberg, B. (1980), "The Happy Worker: Determinants of Job Satisfaction," *American Journal of Sociology* 86 (1980): 247–271.

Griffin, J. (1986), *Well-Being: Its Meaning, Measurement and Moral Importance* (Oxford: Clarendon Press).

Grigsby, J., and D. Stevens (2000), *Neurodynamics of Personality* (New York: Guilford Press).

Halevy, E. (1928), *The Growth of Philosophic Radicalism* (London: Faber and Gwyer).

Hall, R. H. (1986), *Dimensions of Work* (Beverly Hills, CA: Sage).

Harrington, M. (1962), *The Other America: Poverty in the United States* (New York: Macmillan).

Hayek, F. A. (1945), "The Price System as a Mechanism for Using Knowledge," *American Economic Review* 35: 519–530.

Hegel, G. W. F. (1821/1952), *Hegel's Philosophy of Right* (Oxford: Oxford University Press).

Herzberg, F., B. Mausner, and B. Snyderman (1959), *The Motivation to Work* (New York, Wiley).

Himmelfarb, G. (1983), *The Idea of Poverty* (New York: Knopf).

(1991), *Poverty and Compassion: The Moral Imagination of the Late Victorians* (New York: Vintage Books).

Hirschhorn, L. (1997), *Reworking Authority: Leading and Following in the Post-Modern Organization* (Cambridge, MA: MIT Press).

Hirshberg, J. (1998), *The Creative Priority* (New York: HarperCollins).

Hunter, R. (1904/65), *Poverty: Social Conscience in the Progressive Era* (New York: Harper and Row).

Hyatt-Williams, A (1998) *Cruelty, Violence, and Murder: Understanding the Criminal Mind* (London: Karnac Books).

Inglehart, R., and J.-R. Rabier (1986), "Aspirations Adapt to Situations – But Why Are the Belgians So Much Happier than the French?" in F. M. Andrew (ed.), *Research on the Quality of Life* (Ann Arbor, MI: Institute for Social Research).

Inman, Robert (1998) *Old Dogs and Children* (Boston: Little Brown).

International Labor Organization [ILO](1976), *Employment, Growth and Basic Needs: A One-World Problem* (Geneva: ILO).

Jencks, C., L. Perlman, and L. Rainwater (1988), "What Is a Good Job? A New Measure of Labor Market Success," *American Journal of Sociology* 93: 1322–1357.

Juster, F. T. (1985), "Preferences for Work and Leisure," in F. T. Juster and F. P. Stafford (eds.), *Time Goods and Well-Being* (Ann Arbor, MI: Survey Research Center, Institute for Social Research).

Juster, F. T., and P. N. Courant (1986), "Integrating Stocks and Flows in Quality of Life Research," in Frank M. Andrews (ed.), *Research on the Quality of Life* (Ann Arbor, MI: Institute for Social Research).

Juster, F. T., and F. P. Stafford (1985), *Time, Goods and Well-Being* (Ann Arbor, MI: Institute for Social Research).

Katz, M. (1989) *The Undeserving Poor* (New York: Pantheon Books).

Kilpatrick, R. W. (1973), "The Income Elasticity of the Poverty Line," *Review of Economics and Statistics* 55: 327–332.

Klein, Melanie. (1937/1964) "Love, Guilt and Reparation," in Melanie Klein and Joan Riviere (eds.), *Love, Hate and Reparation* (New York: W. W. Norton).

Kohn, M., and C. Schooler (1983), *Work and Personality: An Inquiry into the Impact of Social Stratification* (Norwood, NJ: Ablex).

Kohut, H. (1977), *The Restoration of the Self* (New York: International Universities Press).

(1986), "Forms and Transformations of Narcissism," in A. Morrison (ed.), *Essential Papers on Narcissism* (New York: New York University Press).

Korunka, C., A. Weiss, K. H. Huemer, and B. Karetta (1995), "The Effect of New Technologies on Job Satisfaction and Psychosomatic Complaints," *Applied Psychology* 44: 123–142.

Kubie, L. (1978), *Symbol and Neurosis* (New York: International Universities Press).

Lane, R. E. (1991), *The Market Experience* (Cambridge: Cambridge University Press).

Langholm, O. (1979), *Price and Value in the Aristotelian Tradition* (New York: Columbia University Press).

Lea, S. E. G., R. M. Tarpy, and P. Webley (1987) *The Individual in the Economy: A Textbook of Economic Psychology* (Cambridge: Cambridge University Press).

Lear, J. (1990), *Love and its Place in Nature: A Philosophical Interpretation of Freudian Psychoanalysis* (New York: Noonday Press).

Lebergott, S. (1968), "Labor Force and Employment Trends," in E. B. Sheldon and W. E. Moore (eds.), *Indicators of Social Change* (New York: Sage).

Levine, D. P. (1988), *Needs, Rights and the Market* (Boulder, CO: Lynne Rienner Publishers).

(1995), *Wealth and Freedom* (Cambridge: Cambridge University Press).

(1998), *Subjectivity in Political Economy* (London: Routledge).

(1999a), "The Capacity for Ethical Conduct," *Psychoanalytic Studies* 1: 73–85.

(1999b), "Creativity and Change," *American Behavioral Scientist* 43: 225–244.

(2001), *Normative Political Economy: Subjective Freedom, the Market, and the State* (London: Routledge).

(2002), "Tolerating Difference and Coping with the Infidel," *Journal for the Psychoanalysis of Culture and Society* 7: 43–53.

Lipset, S. (1990), "American Values and the Market System," in T. Dye (ed.), *The Political Legitimacy of Markets and Government* (Greenwich, CT: JAI Press).

Little, D. (2003), *The Paradox of Wealth and Poverty* (Boulder, CO: Westview).

Loewald, H. (1980), *Papers on Psychoanalysis* (New Haven, CT: Yale University Press).

Mahler, M., F. Pine, and A. Bergman (1975), *The Psychological Birth of the Human Infant: Symbiosis and Individuation* (New York: Basic Books).

Maker, W. (1994), *Philosophy Without Foundations* (Albany, NY: SUNY Press).

Malthus, T. R. (1798), *Essay on the Principle of Population*. 1st edn (London: J. Johnson).

(1872), *Essay on the Principle of Population*. 7th edn (London: Reeves and Turner).

Mandeville, B. (1714/1924), *The Fable of the Bees* (Oxford: Clarendon).

Marshall, A. (1890), *Principles of Economics*, 8th edn (London: Macmillan).

(1895), *Principles of Economics*, 3rd edn (London: Macmillan).

Marshall, T. H. (1981), *The Right to Welfare and Other Essays* (New York: Free Press).

Marx, K. (1964), *Karl Marx: Early Writings* (New York: McGraw-Hill).

(1967). *Capital*, vol. I (New York: International Publishers).

(1973), *Grundrisse* (New York: Vintage).

(1977a), *Capital*, vol. I (New York: Vintage Books)

(1977b), *Karl Marx: Selected Writings*, ed. D. McLellan (Oxford: Oxford University Press).

Maslow, A. (1943), "A Theory of Human Motivation," *Psychology Review* 50: 376–396.

Mayer, S. E. (1997), *What Money Can't Buy: Family Income and Children's Life Chances* (Cambridge, MA: Harvard University Press).

Mollat, M. (1986), *The Poor in the Middle Ages* (New Haven, CT: Yale University Press).

Murray, Charles (1995). *Losing Ground: American Social Policy, 1950–1980* (New York: Basic Books).

Nussbaum, M. C. (1995), "Human Capabilities, Female Human Beings," in M. Nussbaum and J. Glover (eds.), *Women, Culture and Development: A Study of Human Capabilities* (Oxford: Clarendon Press).

(2001), "Adaptive Preferences and Women's Options," *Economics and Philosophy* 17: 67–88.

Nussbaum, M. C., and A. K. Sen (eds.) (1993), *The Quality of Life* (Oxford: Clarendon Press).

Orshansky, M. (1965), "Counting the Poor: Another Look at the Poverty Profile," *Social Security Bulletin* 28: 3–29.

(1969), "How Poverty is Measured," *Monthly Labor Review* 92: 37–41.

Petty, W. (1662/1986), *A Treatise of Taxes and Contributions*, in C. Hull (ed.), *The Economic Writings of Sir William Petty*, vol. I (Fairfield, NJ: Augustus Kelley).

Pogge, T. W. (2001), "Eradicating Systemic Poverty: Brief for a Global Resources Dividend," *Journal of Human Development* 2: 59–77.

Polanyi, K. (1957a), "Aristotle Discovers the Economy," in K. Polanyi *et al.* (eds.), *Trade and Market in the Early Empires* (Glencoe: The Free Press).

(1957b), *The Great Transformation: The Political and Economic Origins of our Time* (Boston: Beacon Press).

Poynter, J. R. (1969), *Society and Pauperism: English Ideas on Poor Relief, 1795–1834* (New York: Routledge).

Ricardo, D. (1815/1951–73), *Essay on the Influence of a Low Price of Corn on the Profits of Stock*, in P. Sraffa (ed.), *Works and Correspondence of David Ricardo*, vol. IV (Cambridge: Cambridge University Press).

(1817/1951–73), *Principles of Political Economy*, in P. Sraffa (ed.), *Works and Correspondence of David Ricardo* (Cambridge: Cambridge University Press).

Roll, E. (1953), *A History of Economic Thought* (Englewood Cliffs, NJ: Prentice-Hall).

Ross, C. E., and M. Van Willigen (1997), "Education and the Subjective Quality of Life," *Journal of Health and Social Behavior* 38: 275–297.

Rostow, W. W. (1960), *The Stages of Economic Growth* (Cambridge: Cambridge University Press).

Rowntree, B. S. (1941), *Poverty and Progress: A Second Social Survey of York* (London: Longmans).

Rowntree, B. S., and G. R. Lavers (1951), *Poverty and the Welfare State: A Third Social Survey of York* (London: Longmans).

Sabel, C. (1982), *Work and Politics: The Division of Labor in Industry* (New York: Cambridge University Press).

Sahlins, M. (1988), *Stone Age Economics* (New York: Routledge).

(1995), *How Natives Think* (Chicago: University of Chicago Press).

Schultz, T. W. (1993), *The Economics of Being Poor* (Oxford: Blackwell).

Scitovsky, T. (1977). *The Joyless Economy: An Inquiry into Human Satisfaction and Consumer Dissatisfaction* (New York: Oxford University Press).

Sen, A. K. (1987), *The Standard of Living: The Tanner Lectures* (Cambridge: Cambridge University Press).

(1999), *Development as Freedom* (New York: Knopf).

Smith, A. (1937), *Wealth of Nations* (New York: Modern Library).

Smith, T. (1995), "Public Support for Public Spending, 1973–1994," *The Public Perspective* 6: 1–3.

Smolensky, E., and R. Plotnick (1993), "Inequality and Poverty in the United States: 1900–1990," Institute for Research on Poverty Discussion Paper No. 998–93.

Spenner, K. I. (1979), "Temporal Change in Work Content," *American Sociological Review* 44: 968–975.

(1983), "Prometheus Deciphered: The Skill Level of Work," *American Sociological Review* 48: 824–837.

Spitz, R. (1965), *The First Year of Life* (New York: International Universities Press).

Stern, D. (1985), *The Interpersonal World of the Infant* (New York: Basic Books).

Stewart, F. (1985), *Planning to Meet Basic Needs* (London: Macmillan).

Streeten, S. J. Burki, M. Haq, N. Hicks, and F. Stewart (1981), *First Things First: Meeting Basic Needs in Developing Countries* (London: Oxford University Press).

Tawney, R. H. (1962), *Religion and the Rise of Capitalism* (Gloucester, MA: Peter Smith).

Thompson, E. P. (1963), *The Making of the English Working Class* (London: Golancz).

(1993), "The Moral Economy of the English Crowd in the Eighteenth Century," in *Customs in Common* (New York: New Press: 185–258).

Todorov, T. (1984), *The Conquest of America*, trans. Richard Howard (New York: Harper and Row).

Townsend, J. (1786/1971), *Dissertation on the Poor Laws* (Berkeley, CA: University of California Press).

Tversky, A., and D. Kahneman (1981), "The Framing of Decisions and the Psychology of Choice," *Science* 211 (30 January): 435–458.

Wachtel, Paul L. (1983), *The Poverty of Affluence: A Psychological Portrait of the American Way of Life* (New York: Free Press).

Webb, S., and B. Webb (1963), *English Poor Law History* (Hamden, Connecticut: Archon Books).

Weber, M. (1992), *The Protestant Ethic and the Spirit of Capitalism*, trans. T. Parsons (London: Routledge).

Winnicott, D. (1960a/1965), "The Theory of the Parent-Infant Relationship," in *The Maturational Process and the Facilitating Environment* (Madison, CT: International Universities Press, 1965).

(1960b/1965), "Ego Distortions in Terms of True and False Self," in *The Maturational Process and the Facilitating Environment* (Madison, CT: International Universities Press, 1965).

(1971), "The Use of an Object and Relating Through Identifications," in *Playing and Reality* (London: Routledge).

(1986), *Home Is Where We Start From* (New York: W. W. Norton & Co.).

Witter, R. A., M. A. Okun, W. A. Stock, and M. J. Haring (1984), "Education and Subjective Well-being: a Meta-analysis," *Education Evaluation and Policy Analysis* 6: 165–173.

Wolf, E. (1988), *Treating the Self: Elements of Clinical Self Psychology* (New York: Guilford Press).

Yeatman, A. (2003), "Individualized Citizenship and Service Delivery" (unpublished paper).

# Index